EYTSEN Technical P

SPECIAL EDUCATIONAL NEEDS IN THE EARLY YEARS: PRIMARY SCHOOL ENTRY UP TO THE END OF YEAR 1

AUTHORS:

Pam Sammons
Rebecca Smees
Brenda Taggart
Kathy Sylva
Edward Melhuish
Iram Siraj-Blatchford
Karen Elliot

Acknowledgements

The EYTSEN Project draws on the data collected as part of the Effective Provision of Pre-School Education (EPPE) Project, a longitudinal study funded by the DfES. The research would not have been possible without the support and cooperation of the six Local Authorities and many pre-school centres and primary schools, children and parents involved. We wish to record the important contribution made by the regional research officers: Anne Dobson, Isabella Hughes, Marjorie Jeavons, Margaret Kehoe, Kate Lewis, Maria Morahan, Sharon Sadler and our part time research assistants. We are grateful to Professor Ingrid Lunt for her helpful comments on earlier drafts.

THE EPPE/EYTSEN RESEARCH TEAM

Principal Investigators

Professor Pam Sammons
Institute of Education, University of London

Brenda Taggart
Research Co-ordinator
Institute of Education, University of London

Professor Kathy Sylva
Department of Educational Studies, University of Oxford

Professor Edward Melhuish
Institute for the Study of Children, Families and Social Issues, Birkbeck, University of London

Professor Iram Siraj-Blatchford
Institute of Education, University of London

Senior Research Officers for Statistical Analyses
Rebecca Smees
Institute of Education, University of London

Karen Elliot
Institute of Education, University of London

Published in May 2004 by the Institute of Education University of London
20 Bedford Way, London WC1H OAL

Pursuing Excellence in Education

ISBN 085473 681 6

Ricoh Document Management. London.

The views expressed in this report are the authors' and do not necessarily reflect those of the Department for Education and Skills.

CONTENTS

page

SUMMARY AND CONCLUSION 39

EXECUTIVE SUMMARY

The Early Years Transition and Special Educational Needs (EYTSEN) research builds on the work of the Effective Provision of Pre-School Education (EPPE) project, a major longitudinal study of a national sample of young children's progress and development through pre-school and into primary school until the end of Key Stage 1 (age 3+ to 7 years) (Sylva et al 1999).[1] The Department for Education & Skills (DfES) funds both the EPPE and EYTSEN research. The EYTSEN study focuses on special educational needs (SEN). It explores evidence of possible SEN amongst pre-school children and follows their progress from entry to the study up to the end of Year 1. It uses a range of information to identify children who may be 'at risk' in terms of either cognitive or social/behavioural development and investigates links with a variety of child, parent and family characteristics, including multiple disadvantage and the home learning environment. It also explores the identification of SEN amongst the sample at school and parents' perceptions of whether their child has SEN and what provision their child received. A summary report (and research brief) of the EYTSEN research is available from the DfES[2].

Information for over 2800 children attending 141 pre-school centres selected from five regions across England has been analysed. Centres in the study were drawn from a range of types of pre-school providers (local authority day nurseries, integrated or combined centres (which combined education and care), playgroups, private day nurseries, nursery schools and nursery classes). One-to-one assessments of different aspects of young children's cognitive development were conducted by trained researchers at entry to the study (age three years plus) and later at entry to primary school. Further follow up was conducted at the end of Year 1, when class teachers assessed children's Reading and Mathematics attainment. In addition, ratings of individual children's social and behavioural development were made by pre-school workers when children entered the pre-school study, and by teachers when children enter primary school, and again in Year 1. We thus have several sources of information that can be used to explore young children's cognitive attainment and progress and their social/behavioural development over several years. A further 'home' sample of 314 children joined the study at entry to primary school. These children were included because they had little or no pre-school experience. The inclusion of these children allows comparison of children who had attended a pre-school and those who did not experience such group care. This paper reports on the extent to which 'home' children were found to be 'at risk' of SEN at entry to primary school.

In addition to child assessments, parental interviews conducted when children entered the pre-school study were used to collect detailed information about childcare history and health, and characteristics of children, their families and home environments. Follow up questionnaires, which included a section on SEN, were distributed to parents when children were in primary school providing additional information to the study.

The results of analyses of information about children identified as 'at risk' of SEN in the pre-school period (age 3 years to rising 5) up to the start of primary school and the influence of type of pre-school attended has been reported in EYTSEN Technical Paper 1. This paper follows up the same sample of children and focuses on the identification of children 'at risk' of SEN and those who have been identified by teachers at primary school as showing some form of SEN. It describes attainment patterns in Reading and Mathematics assessed by standardized group tests at the end of Year 1 and explores variations in social behaviour. It also reports on the characteristics of children identified as 'at risk' of SEN by the research and also examines the characteristics of those identified by schools as showing SEN. An accompanying paper (EYTSEN Technical Paper 3) focuses on information from a parental questionnaire survey, which explored parents' views and experiences of SEN.

---

[1] Full details about the sample in the main EPPE study is given in a series of EPPE Technical Papers (listed in Appendix 2).
[2] The summary report and research brief are available on the DfES website (www.dfes.gov.uk/research).

Aims of the EYTSEN project

The EYTSEN study investigates the concept and identification of SEN amongst young children, recognising that such needs can be viewed as social constructs, and that some aspects of need may be seen as particular points along a developmental continuum. Children may be perceived differently by parents, pre-school workers and teachers (Hay et al., 1999; Heiser et al., 2000). At some stages children may be identified as giving cause for concern or be seen to show particular 'needs' but not at others. Likewise different adults may have different understandings or perceptions of SEN. Young children develop differently so changes in status in terms of 'need' may be expected to take place between the ages of 3 and 6 years, the period covered in the EYTSEN research (for further discussion of the issues surrounding the identification of SEN for young children see Scott and Carran (1989) and Roffey (1999)). Change over time, in children's status, cannot be attributed directly to pre-school or other interventions unless a randomised controlled trial (RCT) is conducted. The children in the ETYSEN project were not involved in an experiment or RCT but rather represent naturally occurring variation among a national sample of children attending different types of pre-school provision. In contrast to an experimental design, the EYTSEN analysis provides a more accurate picture of variation in young children's cognitive attainments and progress and their social/behavioural development during the pre-school period and up to the end of Year 1 of primary school.

It is recognised that both *definitions of* and *criteria for, the identification* of SEN are contested concepts. The EYTSEN study pays particular attention to exploration of evidence of possible SEN using a variety of definitions and attempts to identify different categories of possible 'risk'. It seeks to address three main research objectives:

1   To examine the impact of different pre-school settings on the progress and development of, children who may be seen as vulnerable or 'at risk' of developing 'Special Educational Needs' over the pre-school period and in transition to school until the end of Year 1, including:

   • identifying and describing the characteristics of those children who fall into potential 'at risk' categories, using a range of information including cognitive assessments, pre-school staff assessments of social behaviour and parental interviews at different ages during the early years of care and education in pre-school and primary school (3 years+, rising 5 years and 6years);

   • analysing the distribution of 'at risk' groups across different types of pre-school provider.

   • describing the patterns of progress and changes in cognitive and social/behavioural development of the various 'at risk' groups across the pre-school period to the end of KS1.

2   To identify pre-school centres' policies and practice in relation to the early identification of SEN as reported by centre managers.

3   To examine the relationships between pre-school centre quality characteristics and the subsequent progress and development of different 'at risk' groups up to the end of Year 1.

EYTSEN Technical Paper 1 focused on the pre-school period. This report follows up the progress and development of the sample of children during KS1 up to the end of Year 1 and explores the characteristics of children identified as showing some form of SEN at school and their movement in and out of 'risk'. It also explores the attainment and 'risk' status of children with little or no pre-school experience at entry to primary school (a 'home' sample) and, at the end of Year 1, and investigates whether quality of pre-school has a continuing impact on children's attainment and social/behavioural outcomes. The extent to which different groups of children in the sample are identified as showing SEN at school, and whether this matches definitions of 'at risk' status during pre-school is also explored.

The SEN Code of Practice (DfES, 2001) provides the following definition of SEN:

"Children have special educational needs if they have a learning difficulty which calls for special educational provision to be made for them.
Children have a learning difficulty if they:
a)   have more significant delay in learning than children of the same age or
b)   have a disability which prevents or hinders them from making use of educational facilities generally provided for children of the same age in schools within the area of the local education authority
c)   are under compulsory school age and fall within the definitions   a) or b) above, or would do so if special educational provision was not made for them.
Children must not be regarded as having a learning difficulty solely because the language or form of language of their home is different from the language in which they will be taught."
(DfES, 2001; p6)

The Code of Practice focuses on cognitive attainment, but a child may receive a statement of SEN if their behaviour is such that it is affecting their attainment potential. The Code of Practice (2001) stresses the benefits of early identification of needs.

The EYTSEN project examines the concept of SEN within a framework of potential 'risk', rather than attempting to identify a fixed cognitive or social/behavioural problem. Both cognitive and social/behavioural measures of young children's development are analysed to explore the relationships between the two and to acknowledge the need to look at multiple outcomes within the education and care system and their association with different child, parent and family characteristics. In addition, the characteristics of those children who are identified at school as showing SEN are investigated.

The definition of 'at risk' status

Developing a robust definition of children who may be considered to be most 'at risk' of showing some form of SEN is an important component of the EYTSEN study. Information has been analysed to explore the range in young children's cognitive attainment and social/behavioural development at three different time points:

- Entry to a pre-school in the sample (a target pre-school centre), age three years plus;
- Entry to primary school, age rising five years;
- End of Year 1.

Several measures were used because it is recognised that individual children's attainments can vary in different areas of learning and development. At school, low attainment in specific areas of the curriculum may require additional forms of learning support and may be used in the identification of SEN. Aspects of both cognitive and social/behavioural development were addressed.

Measures of children's General Cognitive Ability (GCA) covering both verbal and non-verbal components were collected at entry to pre-school and also at entry to primary school. These were based on one to one assessments using the British Ability Scales (BAS II, Elliot et al, 1996) In addition measures of children's attainments in Pre-Reading and Early Number Concepts were collected at entry to primary school. At the end of Year 1 children were assessed on Reading and Mathematics using the Primary Reading Test (France NFER-NELSON, 1978) and Mathematics 6 (Hague et al. NFER-NELSON, 1997)

Social/behavioural development is also highly relevant to the identification of possible SEN. At pre-school staff completed the Adaptive Social Behavioural Inventory (ASBI), a 30 item checklist, for each child in the sample (Hogan et al., 1992). At primary school, the child's class teacher completed an expanded version of the ASBI (Child Social Behavioral Questionnaire). At the end of Year 1, staff completed selected items from the Child Social Behavioral Questionnaire and also the Goodman Strengths and Difficulties Questionnaire (SDQ) (Goodman, 1997).

The definition of possible 'at risk' status used, was children whose score was one standard deviation or more below the mean. At each time point this was investigated in comparison to national norms and also EPPE sample assessment scores. For the GCA it is possible to make comparisons with the national mean. The results indicated that, at entry to the study, a substantial proportion of EPPE children were significantly below the national average (around a third), a much higher proportion than would be expected, a reflection of the weighting of the sample towards disadvantaged groups. This feature of the sample increases the chances of identifying children 'at risk' of possible SEN in national terms, because of known links between social disadvantage and the incidence of SEN. In addition, a more stringent definition (1 sd below EPPE sample mean) provides an additional indicator of those at 'strong cognitive risk'.

For social/behavioural development the EYTSEN study focussed on two important areas - Peer Sociability and Anti-social/worried/upset behaviour derived from ASBI ratings (see EPPE Technical Paper 7 for details of these dimensions of behaviour) at entry to the study and again at entry to primary school. At the end of Year 1, three scales from the Goodman instrument were selected as specially relevant to the study of SEN: Peer problems, Emotional symptoms and Conduct problems. This report utilises the following sources of information:

• First parent interview completed when children entered the study (for background details);
• Child cognitive and social/behavioural assessments from three time points;
• Teachers' records of child's SEN status carried out when child was in Year 1.

An index of multiple disadvantage was created based on child, parent and home environment characteristics associated with 'at risk' status.

The sample
In summer 2002 the youngest cohort of children in the study (cohort 4) took their end of Year 1 assessments. The sample used in this report was all those children for whom we had received Year 1 data by September 2002[3]. In total, 91% of the main pre-school child sample (i.e. not including the 'home' children with little or no pre-school experience), had information from entry to the study and the end of Year 1. Slightly smaller numbers had a behavioural assessment (86%). Of the 'home' children with little or no pre-school experience, assessments were available for approximately 90% of children for entry to primary school and the end of Year 1 assessments.

Table i: Proportion of main sample at entry to Primary school with cognitive or Behavioural data at the end of Year 1

% of original sample	Tracked child with any information	At least one cognitive assessment	Behavioural assessment
Main sample (n=2857)			
Entry to primary school	95.4	95.4*[4]	95.8
End of Year 1	91.1	90.9	85.9

---

[3] A slightly larger sample was used for the contextualised multilevel analyses in section 2, as more data was available by that stage.

[4] 93.7% of children had enough cognitive assessments to create their overall GCA.

Table ii: Proportion of 'home' sample tracked from entry to primary school to the end of Year 1

	Tracked child with any information	At least one cognitive assessment	Behavioural assessment
No pre-school experience sample *The 'home' group (n=314)* End of Year 1	90.4	89.8	88.9

KEY FINDINGS

This section is a summary of the key findings from this paper, in relation to the main EYTSEN research objectives. Research objective 2 has been addressed in an earlier technical report (EYTSEN Technical Paper 1).

Research Objective 1

To examine the impact of different types of pre-school centres on the progress and development of children who may be seen as vulnerable or 'at risk' of developing 'Special Educational Needs' over the pre-school period and up to the end of Year 1. This includes:

- *The identification and description of the characteristics of those children who fall into potential 'at risk' categories, using a range of information including cognitive assessments, pre-school staff assessments of social behaviour and parental interviews at different ages during the early years of care and education in pre-school and primary school (3 years plus, rising 5 years and 6 years).*

- *An analysis of the distribution of 'at risk' groups across different types of pre-school provider.*

- *A description of patterns of progress and changes in cognitive and social/behavioural development of the various 'at risk' groups across the pre-school period to the end of KS1.*

Overlap between different definitions of 'at risk' status:
- *Reading and Mathematics assessments at the end of Year 1*

In total, 7% of children were identified as 'at risk' on both the Mathematics and the Reading assessment at the end of Year 1. Approximately half of the children found to be 'at risk' on either the Reading or Mathematics assessment were also classified as 'at risk' on the other cognitive assessment. This is in line with the findings about children classified as 'at risk' at the previous two time points (age 3 years plus and at rising 5 years when children started primary school). It suggests that a small group of children are experiencing multiple cognitive problems, and that being 'at risk' on one cognitive area increases significantly the likelihood of being 'at risk' on the other.

- *Cognitive (Reading and Mathematics assessments) and social/behavioural 'risk' at the end of Year 1*

A moderate relationship between individual social/behavioural measures and Reading/Mathematics 'risk' was evident at the end of Year 1. Again this finding is in line with the associations found during the pre-school period. Approximately one quarter of those 'at risk' on cognitive outcomes were also 'at risk' on an individual social/behavioural outcome such as Peer or Conduct problems. When the social/behavioural scales are added together to create an index of behavioural 'risk' (using all five scales for the Goodman SDQ) over two thirds of children identified as 'at risk' in terms of low Reading attainment at age 6 years plus were also found to be 'at risk' on at least one social/behavioural scale. A similar pattern was found for Mathematics.

These results show that cognitive and social/behavioural 'risk' tends to be associated in Key Stage 1 but reveals that the type of social/behavioural 'risk' may vary.

Movement in and out of 'at risk' status

The proportion of children who remain 'at risk' over three time points (entry to the study, entry to primary school and the end of Year 1) is small. For Reading and Mathematics assessments, over two thirds of the overall sample of children were not 'at risk' on any of the three time points (68%), 19% were 'at risk' at one time point only, 9% were 'at risk' at two time points. Between three and four percent of children were identified as 'at risk' on all three time points. These children may be the most vulnerable in terms of developing SEN and may require additional support at school.

In terms of stability, children are more likely to remain 'at risk' for the cognitive outcomes than the behavioural outcomes, where movement in and out of 'risk' was more fluid. The one exception is for Conduct problems, where approximately three percent of children were identified as 'at risk' on all three time points. This has possible implications for timing of assessment and intervention. It may be less appropriate to assess Peer and Emotional related symptoms early on in a child's pre-school or primary school experience, but early signs of Conduct problems may be more long-lasting and thus early identification and help may be beneficial.

Table iii: Proportion of main sample 'at risk' at different time points.

	Proportion of children NOT 'at risk' on any time point	Proportion of children 'at risk' on three time points
Reading	68.3%	2.6%
Mathematics	68.7%	3.7%
Emotional symptoms	62.7%	0.6%
Conduct problems	63.5%	3.1%
Peer problems	66.8%	1.8%

Over two time points, primary school entry to the end of Year 1, the proportion of children 'at risk' at both time points is lower than found previously between entry to the study and entry to primary school (see EYTSEN Technical Paper 1). Of the overall child sample, approximately six percent for Reading and eight percent for Mathematics were classified as 'at risk' at both primary school entry and again at the end of Year 1.

Children who made up the small group who were 'at risk' over three time points were much more likely to be multiply disadvantaged than children who were not identified as 'at risk' or found to be 'at risk' on only one, or two time points.

Child, parent and home environment characteristics of children with 'at risk' status

At the end of Year 1 children identified as 'at risk' of SEN were found to have similar background characteristics to those found at the two earlier time points, at entry to pre-school and at entry to reception (see EYTSEN Technical Paper 1 for details). For the Reading and Mathematics assessments, children 'at risk' were more likely to have mothers having no qualifications, mothers not working and fathers in lower SES groups. Children 'at risk' were also more likely to have poorer home learning environments. Although this relationship was slightly weaker than found at earlier time points, the quality of the home learning environment at entry to the study continued to predict the likelihood of being identified as 'at risk'.

The multiple disadvantage indicator, made up of 10 individual 'risk' indicators collected at entry to the study was still a powerful predictor of cognitive 'at risk' status at the end of Year 1. For example, a quarter of children in the overall sample experienced no disadvantage factor. In contrast this was the case for only 13% of those identified as 'at risk' for Reading and 10% of those identified for Mathematics. A quarter of children in the overall sample experienced three or more disadvantage factors compared to 41% of those identified as 'at risk' for Reading and 44% to of those identified as 'at risk' for Mathematics.

A number of new patterns of 'risk' emerged. At the end of Year 1 significant gender differences in outcomes emerged. Boys were significantly more likely to be identified as 'at risk' for Reading, Mathematics, Peer problems and especially Conduct problems. Of those children identified as 'at risk' for conduct problems, 70% were boys. Although children for whom English as an additional language were still more likely to be identified as 'at risk' for English and Mathematics, they were no longer found to be 'at risk' for any of the social/behavioural outcomes.

As with earlier time points, the social/behavioural outcomes showed a weaker relationship with child background factors in comparison with the associations found for cognitive attainments. Amongst the different social/behavioural dimensions, Conduct problems were most likely to show a significant relationship with background characteristics (including father absent, marital status and multiple disadvantage).

Distribution of 'at risk' children and type of pre-school

Earlier analyses (EYTSEN Technical Paper 1) had indicated that children from integrated (centres combining education and care) provision were more likely to move out of 'risk' over the pre-school period than children from other forms of pre-school provision. It should be noted that integrated (combined) centres also had the highest proportions of children 'at risk' at entry to the study reflecting the more disadvantaged intakes they served

By the end of Year 1 children from integrated centres are still more likely to be identified as being 'at risk', with some of the highest proportions of children 'at risk' for Reading (second highest), Mathematics (highest) and emotional symptoms. However, the proportion of children 'at risk' had reduced from 40% at entry to the study in pre-school (using the most stringent measure of 'risk', of 1 sd below the sample mean) to 17% for Reading and 25% for Mathematics. Of the children attending integrated provision classified as 'at risk' at entry to the study only 6% remained 'at risk' over the next two time points for Reading and 24% for Mathematics. This suggests that integrated provision can have an impact on children's 'risk' status, especially promoting better Reading outcomes. This impact appears to continue up to the end of Year 1.

Children from private day nurseries were the least likely to be classified as 'at risk' at any time point, with 85% of children not 'at risk' for both Mathematics and Reading at any time point. It must be noted that the children from private day nurseries came from the most affluent home backgrounds, who are least likely to be 'at risk'.

The impact of not attending a pre-school centre

Children who had not attended a pre-school centre (the 'home' group) attained significantly poorer cognitive scores than their peers who had attended a pre-school setting, both at entry to primary school and at the end of Year 1. At entry to school, 48% of children with no pre-school experience were identified as 'at risk' on a general ability assessment ('strong cognitive risk' - most stringent measure) compared with only 16% of the main sample. By the end of Year 1, 28% of 'home' children for Reading and 37% for Mathematics were 'at risk' compared with only 13% and only 16% respectively for the main sample. It must be remembered that this 'home' group were generally more disadvantaged than the main sample, and tended to have a greater proportion of children who had English as an additional language. Nonetheless, even when the impact of these background influences was controlled, 'home' children were still significantly more likely to be identified as 'at risk' at both time points. Multilevel analyses found that 'home' children performed significantly below other children for all outcomes except Conduct problems at the end of Year 1. The attainment and social/behavioural gap between 'home' children and those who had attended a pre-school centre showed little sign of closing as children moved through Key Stage 1.

Teacher identification of SEN

Approximately 60% of the children identified by the EYTSEN 'at risk' classification were also identified by teachers as having SEN in the particular subject area or were being monitored for SEN in this area in Year 1. Nonetheless the overlap was not perfect. In general teachers/schools appear to be more likely to identify the lowest attaining children as having SEN. Nonetheless, there was a fairly close correspondence between the research definition of those 'at risk' and schools identification of SEN, and similar types of children (in terms of multiple disadvantage) were found to be over-represented amongst both groups. The results suggest that a more formal definition of potential 'risk' (such as the 1 sd below the mean cut off) could prove a useful screening device to assist schools and teachers in the process of early identification and support. Children who are multiply disadvantaged, have not attended a pre-school centre and who are 'at risk' in terms of scores below a particular 'cut off' could receive extra support and monitoring to ease their transition to primary school and during reception and Year 1.

One important difference between the identification of children 'at risk' and teacher reports of SEN relates to child age. For cognitive attainment it is known that child's age (in months) shows a significant association with attainment. For this reason EYTSEN standardised measures in order to ensure that the influence of developmental age was controlled. It is important to note that EYTSEN provides strong evidence that significantly more children young for their year (summer born children) were identified as having a SEN during Key Stage 1. Overall nearly 34% of summer born children was reported to have a SEN compared with just under 21% of autumn born children (the equivalent figure is 27.5% of spring born children). This finding indicates that primary schools do not take proper account of the influence of developmental age in identifying SEN during the early primary years. Only standardised assessments can enable proper control for age effects. The finding has important implications given current demands that teacher assessment should be given greater weight in schools.

Research Objective 3

> *To examine the relationship between pre-school centre quality characteristics (using the Early Childhood Environmental Rating Scales) and the subsequent progress and development of different 'at risk' groups.*

Measures of pre-school centre quality

The continuing impact of pre-school on child outcomes at the end of Year 1 was measured by three pre-school centre 'quality' instruments (ECERS-R, Harms, Clifford and Cryer, 1998; ECERS-E, Sylva, Siraj-Blatchford, and Taggart, 2003; and CIS, Arnett, 1989 – see EYTSEN Technical Paper 1 for further details). We also used for the first time, measures of centre 'effectiveness' in terms of the amount of progress children made over the pre-school period for different cognitive and social/behavioural outcomes (EPPE Technical Papers 8a and 8b describe how these 'effectiveness' estimates were calculated).

Children who remained 'at risk' for Reading over three time points came from pre-schools with higher levels of recorded 'punitiveness' and 'detachment' in adult-child interaction (measured by the Caregiver Interaction Scale (CIS) and lower overall quality ratings on the Early Childhood Environment Rating Scale (ECERS-R) (see glossary of terms at the end of the paper for a brief description of the quality scales used). The ECERS-R instrument measures care and child-staff interaction. This finding suggests that poorer quality pre-school experience; especially lack of positive staff-child relationships may adversely affect young children's subsequent Reading attainment at school.

In EYTSEN Technical Paper 1, analyses of the pre-school period indicated that the home background characteristics of children attending different types of pre-school settings varied, some serving higher proportions of more disadvantaged young children than others. Nonetheless, when differences in children's background details were taken into account in the statistical analyses, some aspects of centre quality were still found to relate to children's attainment at the end of Year 1 for both English and Mathematics. In terms of centre quality measures, the quality of literacy activities (ECERS-E subscale) and the level of positive interaction between staff and children (ECERS-R subscale) were found to be significantly related to higher Reading attainment at end of Year 1. This was also reflected in the finding that, controlling for background influences, better Year 1 Reading scores were attained by children who had attended pre-school centres that were more effective in promoting children's language development (higher Verbal Value Added scores) during the pre-school period. Although none of the pre-school quality indicators were found to be significantly related to differences in children's attainment in Mathematics in Year 1, higher Mathematics scores in Year 1 were obtained by children who had attended pre-school centres that were more effective in promoting progress in Early Number Concepts (higher Value Added scores) during the pre-school period (For details of the measurement of pre-school centre effectiveness see EPPE Technical Papers 8a & 8b.).

Overview

Taken together these findings suggest that both the quality and effectiveness of the pre-school setting attended continues to have an impact on young children's subsequent cognitive progress during their first years in primary school. 'Home' children and those with relatively short duration or only poor quality pre-school experience are more likely to be classified as 'at risk' and to be identified as showing a SEN during Key Stage 1. The EYTSEN research indicates that high quality pre-school can be viewed as an effective intervention to both reduce the 'risk' of SEN and promote better outcomes for the most vulnerable groups of young children, especially those experiencing multiple disadvantage. In the light of these findings better pre-school provision may be seen as an important component of policies intending to combat social exclusion by providing a better start to school for such vulnerable groups.

The finding that significantly more summer born children (those young for their school year) are reported by schools as showing SEN is also of concern. Research on junior schools in the 1980s found that teachers judged pupils young for their year as of lower ability than their older peers and having more behaviour problems (Mortimore et al, 1988). The EYTSEN findings from a national sample 20 years on indicate that summer born children remain at a disadvantage and are more likely to be viewed as having some form of SEN. The results suggest the need to raise awareness of the impact of developmental age and to ensure that children young for their year receive more support without lowering expectations.

SECTION 1A: The characteristics of children identified as 'at risk' at the end of Year 1 in primary school

Characteristics of children identified as 'at risk' on Cognitive assessments at the end of Year 1

Identifying 'at risk' children on cognitive measures

Children's reading and mathematics attainments were assessed when children were in the summer term of the Year 1 primary year[5]. The assessments used were the Primary Reading Test (France NFER-NELSON, 1978) and Mathematics 6 (Hague et al. NFER-NELSON, 1997). Using nationally age-standardised scores enabled us to compare the performance of the sample with children nationally, as was done previously, at entry to the study and entry to primary school for General Cognitive Ability (GCA). Table 1A.1 shows that the mean for reading is slightly lower than the national average, but this is not the case for mathematics. This section reports results for the main child sample, those with pre-school centre experience who were followed from age 3 years plus to primary school entry. Section 1C focuses in detail on the 'home' sample of children with little or no pre-school centre experience.

Approximately one fifth (22.7%) of the children were 1 standard deviation below the national average on the Primary Reading Test (a score of 85 or below), and 15.6% were 1 standard deviation below for the Mathematics 6 test. This result is in accordance with the conclusion reported in EYTSEN Technical Paper 1 that children who have experienced pre-school tend to make cognitive gains and that the attainment gap narrows (at entry to pre-school it was found that a third of the sample were 1 sd below the national mean in terms of cognitive ability, whereas by entry to primary school the percentage below national norms had reduced to just over a fifth). For mathematics the sample's attainments are up to national norms, though for reading results are still slightly below by the end of Year 1. These results suggest that early gains made over the pre-school, period by children who attended pre-school are not lost by the end of Year 1 in primary school.

Table 1A.1 Mean and standard deviation for national and EPPE sample

	Mean Score	% 'at risk'
Primary Reading test	97.2 (sd=15.5)	22.7
Mathematics 6	100.4 (sd=15.1)	15.6

National mean =100 (sd=15)

Home background characteristics of children 'at risk' on cognitive measures

As noted above, a slightly larger proportion of children were identified as 'at risk' in reading than in mathematics in relation to national norms. Table 1A.2 shows two different approaches to identification of 'risk' based on cognitive data. It was decided to analyse the 'risk' classifications based on the sample means in this section, because this is a more stringent measure and allows comparison with analyses over the pre-school.

---

[5] 56 children took the tests in the autumn term of Year 2. These children scored significantly lower than those who took the tests in the summer term, possibly indicating a 'summer holiday' effect or a high level of absenteeism that meant summer testing was not possible. Age standardized scores were adopted in the EYTSEN analyses.

Table 1A.2 Classifications of 'at risk' status for cognitive Year 1 attainment measures

'Risk' type	Explanation of assessment
Primary Reading test -sample	1 standard deviation below sample mean N=314, score of 82 or below
Mathematics 6 test - sample	1 standard deviation below sample mean N=375, score of 85 or below

The child, family and home environment background characteristics investigated in this section use information collected from the first parent interview for a number of reasons. Firstly, to keep consistency with results for the pre-school period reported in the earlier EYTSEN Technical Paper 1. Secondly, to investigate the impact of early family background on later 'at risk' status. And thirdly, to maximise the sample size, as the second parent questionnaire has a slightly lower return rate than the first parent interview[6]. This paper has concentrated on background factors that show a significant relationship with 'risk' status at the end of Year 1 (whilst keeping consistency between the cognitive and social/behavioural sections).

In total, 7.3% of children were identified as 'at risk' in cognitive development for both the reading and mathematics assessments at the end of Year 1. This means that the overlap between the reading and mathematics 'at risk' classifications is partial, with approximately half of those identified on one assessment also identified as 'at risk' on the other. For example, 56.9% of children found to be 'at risk' on the mathematics assessment were also found to be 'at risk' for reading assessments, and 46.8% of children 'at risk' for reading were also 'at risk' for the mathematics assessment. Children identified as having particularly low attainments on both assessments in Year 1 may be seen to be most vulnerable in terms of showing SEN and subsequent sections will establish to what extent this most vulnerable group were identified at primary school as having a SEN.

• **Gender**

More boys were identified as 'at risk' than girls for both reading and mathematics; however, reading shows the largest gender gap in terms of percentage 'at risk'. Only 40% of those 'at risk' for reading were girls.

Table 1A.3 Gender and percentage of children identified as 'at cognitive risk' at the end of Year 1

	All children	Primary Reading 'risk'	Mathematics 'risk'
Male	52.2	59.9	57.1
Female	47.8	40.1	42.9
Chi-square	--	$X^2 = 8.685$, $p<0.01$	$X^2 = 5.072$, $p<0.05$

• **Ethnic group**

Relatively few ethnic differences in cognitive attainment were found at the end of Year 1. Given the small numbers involved for some minority groups, any differences should be interpreted with considerable caution. The White UK heritage group were slightly under-represented in the 'at risk' group for both reading and mathematics. The Pakistani and Mixed heritage groups were slightly over-represented in the 'at risk' groups for reading and mathematics (although the difference was not statistically significant for mathematics). The white European group were also found to be 'at risk' for reading slightly more than other groups.

---

[6] The first parent interview collected on entry to the study had a return rate of nearly 98%, the second parent questionnaire had a response rate of nearly 84%.

Table 1A.4 Ethnicity and percentage of children identified as 'at cognitive risk' at the end of Year 1

	All children		Primary Reading 'risk'		Mathematics 'risk'	
	%	n	%	n	%	n
White UK heritage	76.5	1863	68.8	216	71.2	267
White Euro heritage	4.1	100	6.1	19	4.0	15
Black Caribbean heritage	3.7	89	3.2	10	4.0	15
Black African heritage	2.1	50	2.5	8	2.4	9
Black – Other	0.7	16	1.3	4	1.1	4
Indian	1.9	47	1.3	4	2.1	8
Pakistani	2.2	54	4.8	15	4.0	15
Bangladeshi	0.7	17	1.3	4	0.8	3
Chinese	0.2	4	0.3	1	0.0	0
Other	1.7	42	2.5	8	2.1	8
Mixed heritage	6.2	151	7.6	24	7.7	29
White non Euro heritage	0.1	2	0.0	0	0.3	1
Unknown	0.1	0	0.3	1	0.3	1
Chi-square	--		$X^2 = 25.448$, p<0.01		ns	

• English as an Additional language (EAL)

As might be anticipated, children for whom English is an additional language (the EAL group) still have a somewhat higher incidence of 'risk' for reading and mathematics by end of Year 1. However, the differences are smaller than those found in terms of cognitive ability at entry to primary school. This suggests that during reception and the first year in primary school, children for whom English is an additional language who attended pre-school continue to make cognitive gains, in comparison with their relative position at entry to pre-school (age 3 years plus).

Table 1A.5 Child's language and percentage of children identified as 'at cognitive risk' at the end of Year 1

	All children	Primary Reading 'risk'	Mathematics 'risk'
English	92.5	85.7	87.7
English not 1st language	7.5	14.3	12.3
Chi-square	--	$X^2 = 24.749$, p<0.001	$X^2 = 15.249$, p<0.001

• Mother's highest qualification level

The percentage of children identified as 'at risk' for cognitive attainment at the end of Year 1 in relation to mother's highest qualification level was little changed from that evident at primary school entry. Children whose mothers reported they had no qualifications were significantly over-represented while those whose mothers had degrees were significantly under-represented in the 'at risk' groups. These consistent findings highlight the importance of maternal education as a continuing predictor of young children's cognitive development. Having a mother with no qualifications nearly doubles the chances that a child will be identified as 'at risk' in Year 1.

Table 1A.6 Mother's qualification and percentage of children identified as 'at cognitive risk' at the end of Year 1

	All children	Primary Reading 'risk'	Mathematics 'risk'
None	17.7	32.8	33.1
16yr vocational	2.0	1.9	3.2
16 academic	37.5	37.3	38.7
18 vocational	12.8	13.4	12.3
18 academic	8.6	4.8	5.6
Degree or equivalent	13.1	5.1	4.3
Higher degree	4.7	1.6	0.3
Other professional	0.7	0.3	0.0
Other miscellaneous	0.7	0.0	0.0
Unknown	2.2	2.9	2.7
Chi-square	--	$X^2 = 81.585$, p<0.001	$X^2 = 119.260$, p<0.001

• Mother's employment status

The association between mother's employment status and low cognitive scores identified during the pre-school period also remains stable. Those whose mothers reported they were not employed when their child was at pre-school were somewhat over represented in the 'at risk' groups for both reading and mathematics at the end of Year 1. It should be noted that differences in employment status are related to mothers' qualification levels with proportionately more mothers who have no qualifications reporting that they were not working.

Table 1A.7 Mother's employment status and percentage of children identified as 'at cognitive risk' at the end of Year 1

	All children	Primary Reading 'risk'	Mathematics 'risk'
Not employed	46.5	58.0	62.7
Employed full time	16.2	10.8	9.1
Employed part time	31.0	24.5	23.2
Self employed	4.1	4.1	2.4
Combination*	0.5	0.0	0.5
Other	0.0	0.0	0.0
Unknown	1.6	2.5	2.1
Chi-square	--	$X^2 = 23.222$, p<0.001	$X^2 = 53.177$, p<0.001

*Part time and self-employed

• Father's SES

Father's socio-economic status, likewise continues to show a significant relationship with 'at risk' status, with a greater proportion of children 'at risk' coming from homes where the father was in a manual occupation, and fewer from homes where the father was in a professional occupation. Those where the father was reported as absent during the pre-school period were also at increased 'risk' of low attainment in Year 1 especially for mathematics.

Table 1A.8 Father's occupation level and percentage of children identified as 'at cognitive risk' at the end of Year 1

		All children	Primary Reading 'risk'	Mathematics 'risk'
Professional	I non manual	8.5	2.2	2.1
Other professional	II non manual	19.4	9.2	8.0
Skilled non man	III non manual	12.6	11.8	13.3
Skilled manual	III manual	22.9	29.3	25.6
Semi skilled	IV manual	11.3	15.9	14.9
Unskilled	V manual	2.2	2.2	3.5
Never worked		0.7	0.3	0.5
Father absent		21.1	27.7	30.4
Unknown		1.3	1.3	1.6
Chi-square		--	$X^2 = 51.975$, p<0.001	$X^2 = 61.071$, p<0.01

• Mother's marital status

Children coming from single parent families were again slightly over represented in the 'at risk' categories, and children coming from families where parents were married and living together were slightly under-represented. This pattern is in line with that found at entry to pre-school and at the start of primary school. It must be remembered that single parents are more likely than families with two parents living together to be multiply disadvantaged in terms of other factors such as employment status, mother's education level etc.

Table 1A.9 Marital status and percentage of children identified as 'at cognitive risk' at the end of Year 1

	All children	Primary Reading 'risk'	Mathematics 'risk'
Never married, single parent	13.3	15.3	17.6
Never married, living with partner	14.4	17.2	17.1
Married, live with spouse	60.0	49.7	48.3
Separated/divorced	10.3	15.9	14.9
Widow/widower	0.2	0.3	0.3
Other	0.5	0.0	0.3
Unknown	1.3	1.6	1.6
Chi-square	--	$X^2 = 21.421$, p<0.001	$X^2 = 28.874$, p<0.001

Home environment characteristics of children 'at risk' on cognitive measures

A measure of the quality of the home learning environment (derived from parents' interview responses about activities with which they engaged with their child such as teaching songs and nursery rhymes, reading to the child, playing with letters and numbers, painting and drawings, visiting the library etc.) showed a strong link with cognitive development at both three years plus and age rising five years. Interestingly, the correlation between the home learning environment and Year 1 cognitive assessments is lower than that found at earlier time points (only 0.14 for reading and mathematics). This may be because the association between the home environment in pre-school and later attainment at school is reduced or may reflect the use of cognitive measures more influenced by school experience. It is likely that details of continued parental activity with their child will be important for attainment at primary school. Information about such aspects has been collected by a follow up parental questionnaire and will be reported separately. However, this early learning activity still shows a statistically significant positive relationship with both higher attainment and lower chance of 'at risk' status in Year 1.

- ### Overall home learning scale
Children with the lowest home learning scores (0-13 range) were still much more likely to be identified as 'at risk' than children with higher scores (a low score in the pre-school period more than doubles the chances of a child being identified as 'at risk' by end Year 1). Similarly, only 5% of 'at risk' children (using reading classification and 4.0% for mathematics) had the highest home learning scale scores (33-45 range), compared with 12.4% for the sample overall.

Table 1A.10 Home learning environment and percentage of children identified as 'at cognitive risk' at the end of Year 1

	All children	Primary Reading 'risk'	Mathematics 'risk'
Mean home learning score	23.6 (sd=7.5)	19.8 (sd=7.5)	20.2 (sd=7.5)
0-13	8.4	19.4	18.7
14-19	20.9	29.3	26.7
20-24	23.6	22.3	22.4
25-32	31.9	21.0	24.0
33-45	12.4	5.1	4.0
Unknown	2.9	2.9	4.3
Chi-square	--	$X^2 = 93.391$, p<0.001	$X^2 = 104.129$, p<0.001

Multiple disadvantage and cognitive 'at risk' status at end of Year 1

EYTSEN created a Multiple Disadvantage index which included 10 indicators in total: three child variables, six parent variables, and one related to the home learning environment (see EYTSEN Technical Paper 1 for details). All the variables were chosen because they related to low baseline attainment at entry to pre-school when looked at in isolation (as described above). The results show that multiple disadvantage remains an important predictor of low cognitive scores and cognitive 'at risk' status at the end of Year in primary 1. Of those children 'at risk' for reading, just under 13% had no multiple disadvantage indicators (compared with nearly 24% of all children). If we compare children with different levels of disadvantage, the relationship between multiple disadvantage and 'risk' is more clearly illustrated.

Table 1A.11 Multiple disadvantage and percentage of children identified as 'at cognitive risk' at the end of Year 1

	All children	Primary Reading 'risk'	Mathematics 'risk'
Mean MD score	1.7 (sd=1.5)	2.5 (sd=1.7)	2.5 (sd=1.6)
0	23.7	12.7	9.6
1-2	47.4	40.4	40.8
3-4	19.8	29.6	32.8
5+	4.8	7.3	11.2
Unknown	4.3	4.5	5.6
Chi-square	--	$X^2 = 80.484, p<0.001$	$X^2 = 120.027, p<0.001$

A further way to analyse the data is to compare the percentages of children in each category of multiple disadvantage who were identified as 'at risk'. For example, of the children experiencing no indicators of disadvantage, only 7.0% were identified as 'at risk' for reading. In contrast, of those children experiencing 5 indicators of disadvantage, nearly a third (32.4%) were identified as 'at risk' for reading.

Characteristics of children identified as 'at risk' on social/behavioural assessments at the end of Year 1

Identifying children 'at risk' on social/behavioural measures

The social/behavioural assessment was carried out in nearly all cases by the child's class teacher in nearly all cases (in some cases a SENCO or learning support assistant completed these), in the summer term of the Year 1 primary[7]. The social/behavioural assessment used was a combination of items from the 'Goodman Strengths and Difficulties Questionnaire' (SDQ), (Goodman, 1997) and the Child Social Behaviour Questionnaire (CSBQ) used at earlier time points in the project. Only Goodman scale items were selected for use in the EYTSEN analysis to allow comparisons with national norms and comparisons with clinical assessments. The five scales that make up the SDQ are listed below with some example items (for full details see Appendix 4)[8]:

The **'Prosocial' scale** e.g. Considerate of other people's feelings. Shares readily with other children.

The **'Hyperactivity'** scale e.g. Restless, overactive, cannot stay still for long. Constantly fidgeting or squirming.

The **'Emotional symptoms' scale** e.g. Often complains of headaches, stomach aches. Many worries, often seems worried.

The **'Conduct problems' scale** e.g. Often has temper tantrums or hot tempers. Generally obedient, usually does what he/she is told.

The **'Peer problems' scale** e.g. Rather solitary, tends to play alone. Has at least one good friend

---

[7] A very small minority of pupils (23) were assessed in the autumn term of Year 2, and some earlier in the summer term (10) making the age range slightly larger. The majority of pupils were between 5 years and 9 months and 6 years and 8 months at the time the assessment took place.
[8] Where there is a mixture of positive and negative statements within the scale the items have been reverse coded.

Comparisons with national norms

Table 1A.12 shows that the scores for the pre-school sample are almost identical to the national levels for all sub-scales (see Meltzer et al. (2000) for further details of national norms). Slightly higher proportions of the pre-school sample were identified as exhibiting 'borderline' or 'abnormal' hyperactive disorders than the national sample, although it must be noted that the national sample includes children up to ten years of age. Goodman scale scores can be classified into normal, borderline or abnormal groupings. An 'abnormal' score can be used to identify children who may experience possible mental disorders (Goodman et al., 2000a & 2000b). The SDQ is also used to discriminate between psychiatric cases and other forms of behaviour difficulty (Goodman & Scott, 1999). The concepts of disorder that underpin the SDQ are based upon the 'Diagnostic and Statistical Manual of Mental Disorders' (4th ed, DSM-IV; American Psychiatric Association, 1994) and 'ICD-10' (World Health Organization, 1994). Children with 'borderline or abnormal' scores have been classified as 'at risk' of SEN in social/behavioural terms for the EYTSEN study.

Table 1A.12 Mean, standard deviation and percentage of children with an identified 'need' (abnormal or borderline) for national and EYTSEN sample

	Sample details 5yrs3mths-7yrs2mths		National details 5-10yrs	
	Mean	(sd)	Mean	(sd)
Goodman Prosocial	7.4	(2.4)	7.3	(2.4)
Goodman Hyperactivity	3.3	(3.0)	3.0	(2.8)
Goodman Emotional symptoms	1.5	(2.0)	1.5	(1.9)
Goodman Conduct problems	1.0	(1.6)	0.9	(1.6)
Goodman Peer problems	1.4	(1.7)	1.4	(1.8)
	%		%	
Goodman Prosocial– borderline or abnormal	25.1		25.3	
Goodman Hyperactivity– borderline or abnormal	23.3		18.9	
Goodman Emotional symptoms– borderline or abnormal	9.4		8.9	
Goodman Conduct problems– borderline or abnormal	14.0		13.2	
Goodman Peer problems– borderline or abnormal	13.1		12.3	
Goodman Prosocial– abnormal	12.0		12.0	
Goodman Hyperactivity– abnormal	17.1		13.8	
Goodman Emotional symptoms– abnormal	5.5		4.8	
Goodman Conduct problems– abnormal	8.3		7.6	
Goodman Peer problems– abnormal	6.7		7.2	

N.B. national norms are not available for smaller age ranges

Table 1A.13 displays the criteria for classifying a child as 'at risk' for the five SDQ scales. As the project aims to look at children potentially 'at risk' of SEN, the children classified as 'borderline' cases were also included in our definition of 'at risk'. Appendix 4 shows the items used to classify 'abnormal' behaviours.

Table 1A.13 Different classifications of 'at risk' status for social/behavioural outcomes

'Risk' type	Explanation of assessment
Goodman Prosocial– borderline or abnormal	25.3% of the national population Number at 'risk'=599, score of 5 or below
Goodman Hyperactivity– borderline or abnormal	18.9% of the national population Number at 'risk' =557, score of 6 or more
Goodman Emotional symptoms– borderline or abnormal	8.9% of the national population Number at 'risk' =225, score of 5 or more
Goodman Conduct problems– borderline or abnormal	13.2% of the national population Number at 'risk' =332, score of 3 or more
Goodman Peer problems– borderline or abnormal	12.3% of the national population Number at 'risk' =313, score of 4 or more

Relationships between different social/behavioural 'at risk' classifications at the end of Year 1

Correlations between the five social/behavioural scales are shown in Table 1A.14 below. The relationships between scores in Pro-social, Hyperactivity and Conduct problem scales are particularly strong (all approximately r=0.6). The Emotional symptoms scale appears to be the most distinct scale with only a moderate relationship with the peer problems scale (r=0.32). The three scales looked at in this section are the 'Emotional symptoms', 'Conduct problems' and 'Peer problems' scales because they relate most strongly to scales reported at earlier time points and are considered most relevant to the identification of 'risk' of SEN[9]. Emotional symptoms and Peer problems showed the strongest relationship to Peer sociability at entry to primary school, and as they represent fairly distinct behaviours, it was decide to use them both for 'risk' classification.

Table 1A.14 Correlations between the five SDQ scales for the EYTSEN sample

	Pro-social	Hyperactivity	Emotional symptoms	Conduct problems	Peer problems
Pro-social		-0.57	-0.10	-0.58	-0.40
Hyperactivity			0.17	0.59	0.33
Emotional symptoms				0.15	0.32
Conduct problems					0.35
Peer problems					

All correlations significant at the 0.01 level

Tables 1A.15-1A.17 assess the degree of overlap between the different 'risk' categories examined in this paper. The overlap between children 'at risk' on the 'Conduct problems' and 'Peer problems' scales show the greatest degree of overlap, with over one third of those identified as being 'at risk' for Conduct problems also being identified as 'at risk' for Peer problems. This group comprises 4.4% of the total sample. Approximately one quarter of those identified as being 'at risk' for Emotional symptoms were also 'at risk' for Peer problems or Conduct problems. Again this group represents only a small proportion of the total sample (3.4%).

Table 1A.15 Conduct problems and peer problems 'risk' classifications

	Not 'at risk' Conduct problems	'at risk' Conduct problems
Not 'at risk' Peer problems	N= 1849	N= 226
'at risk' Peer problems	N= 194	N= 106 (4.4% of whole sample)

It was found that 35.5% of those 'at risk' for Conduct problems were also 'at risk' for peer problems in Year 1

Table 1A.16 Emotional symptoms and peer problems 'risk' classifications

	Not 'at risk' emotional symptoms	'at risk' emotional symptoms
Not 'at risk' Peer problems	N= 1930	N= 143
'at risk' Peer problems	N= 230	N= 82 (3.4% of whole sample)

In all 26.2% of those 'at risk' for emotional symptoms were also 'at risk' for peer problems in Year 1

Table 1A.17 Conduct problems and emotional symptoms 'risk' classifications

	Not 'at risk' Conduct problems	'at risk' Conduct problems
Not 'at risk' emotional symptoms	N= 1871	N= 275
'at risk' emotional symptoms	N= 168	N=57 (2.4% of whole sample)

It was found that 25.3% of those 'at risk' for emotional symptoms are also 'at risk' for Conduct problems in Year 1

---

[9] Correlations between scales at entry to primary school and the end of Year 1: Peer sociability (primary entry) and Peer problems= -0.22, Peer sociability (primary entry) and Emotional symptoms= -0.21, Anti-social/Worried/upset (primary entry) and Conduct problems = 0.39. The Hyperactivity scale was also found to be related to the Anti-social/Worried/upset scale (r=0.37).

Home background characteristics of children identified as 'at risk' on social/behavioural measures

The child, parent and home learning environment characteristics of children identified as 'at risk' for these measures of social behaviour at the end of Year 1 were explored in the same way as at entry to pre-school and entry to school (see EYTSEN Technical Paper 1 for details) to establish whether similar patterns were evident.

• Gender
Boys were much more likely to be identified as 'at risk' for Conduct problems and Peer problems, but no differences between the sexes was found for Emotional symptoms. The gender difference is particularly marked for Conduct problems among this age group with over two thirds of the children identified as 'at risk' being boys.

Table 1A.18 Gender and percentage of children identified as 'at social/behavioural risk' at the end of Year 1

	All children N=2370	'at risk' Emotional symptoms	'at risk' Conduct problems	'at risk' Peer problems
Male	51.9	49.3	69.0	57.5
Female	48.1	50.7	31.0	42.5
Chi square	--	ns	$x^2 = 45.216$, p<0.001	$x^2 = 4.431$, p<0.05

• Ethnic group
There were few significant differences between ethnic groups. Children of Pakistani background were rated as showing slightly more Peer problems. Those of Black Caribbean and mixed heritage were slightly more likely to be identified as 'at risk' for conduct problems, but given the small numbers involved for some minority groups any differences should be interpreted with considerable caution.

Table 1a.19 Ethnic background and percentage of children identified as 'at social/behavioural risk' at the end of Year 1

	All children		'at risk' Emotional symptoms		'at risk' Conduct problems		'at risk' Peer problems	
	%	n	%	n	%	n	%	n
White UK heritage	77.5	1836	76.4	172	70.8	235	74.4	233
White Euro heritage	4.0	94	5.3	12	4.5	15	3.5	11
Black Caribbean heritage	3.8	89	1.8	4	5.7	19	4.2	13
Black African heritage	2.0	47	1.3	3	2.7	9	1.9	6
Black – Other	0.6	14	0.4	1	0.9	3	0.3	1
Indian	1.9	45	2.2	5	1.5	5	2.2	7
Pakistani	2.2	51	3.6	8	2.4	8	4.2	13
Bangladeshi	0.7	16	0.9	2	1.2	4	0.3	1
Chinese	0.1	2	0.0	0	0.0	0	0.0	0
Other	1.4	34	1.3	3	2.4	8	2.2	7
Mixed heritage	5.8	138	6.2	14	7.8	26	6.1	19
White non Euro heritage	0.1	2	0.4	1	0.0	0	0.6	2
Unknown	0.1	2	0.0	0	0.0	0	0.0	0
Chi-square	--		ns		ns		$x^2 = 24.878$, p<0.05	

• English as an Additional language (EAL)

Interestingly, and in contrast to findings at younger age there is no longer any statistically significant association between EAL status and the identification of children 'at risk' in terms of social behaviour.

Table 1A.20 Child's language and percentage of children identified as 'at social/behavioural risk' at the end of Year 1

	All children	'at risk' Emotional symptoms	'at risk' Conduct problems	'at risk' Peer problems
English	93.1	91.6	91.9	92.0
English is an additional language	6.9	8.4	8.1	8.0
Chi-square	--	ns	ns	ns

• Mother's highest qualification level

The analysis of mother's educational level shows that children who's mothers have no qualifications were over-represented in the category 'at risk' for Conduct problems and by contrast children whose mothers had a degree were less likely to be identified as having Conduct problems, but not Peer problems.

Table 1a.21 Mother's qualification level and percentage of children identified as 'at social/behavioural risk' at the end of Year 1

	All children	'at risk' Emotional symptoms	'at risk' Conduct problems	'at risk' Peer problems
None	17.3	21.3	26.5	23.0
16yr vocational	2.1	2.7	3.6	4.2
16 academic	38.1	38.2	33.4	33.9
18 vocational	12.9	8.9	14.8	10.2
18 academic	8.8	8.0	7.8	8.0
Degree or equivalent	12.7	12.4	5.7	14.1
Higher degree	4.6	3.6	3.3	4.2
Other professional	0.7	0.4	0.6	0.6
Other miscellaneous	0.7	0.4	0.0	0.6
Unknown	2.2	4.0	4.2	1.3
Chi-square	--	ns	$X^2 = 46.373$, p<0.001	$X^2 = 18.177$, p<0.05

• Mother's employment status

Children whose mothers worked full time showed fewer emotional symptoms but slightly increased conduct problems. Children whose mothers were employed part-time, however, were under-represented in the 'at risk' group for Conduct problems and to a lesser extent showed lower 'risk' for Peer problems. Those whose mothers were not employed showed an increase 'risk' for Conduct problems (nearly 55% of the 'at risk' group compared to 46% for the whole sample).

These findings differ from those when children were younger, when children whose mothers were not working were only found to be somewhat over-represented in the 'at risk' group for Peer sociability.

Table 1A.22 Mother's employment status and percentage of children identified as 'at social/behavioural risk' at the end of Year 1

	All children	Emotional symptoms	Conduct problems	Peer problems
Not employed	46.2	47.1	54.5	51.4
Employed full time	16.3	14.7	18.7	16.6
Employed part time	31.4	30.7	19.6	26.5
Self employed	3.9	4.0	4.2	4.2
Combination*	0.5	0.4	0.0	0.3
Other	0.0	0.0	0.0	0.0
Unknown	1.6	3.1	3.0	1.0
Chi-square	--	ns	$X^2 = 26.52, p<0.001$	ns

* Part time and self-employed

• Father's social class

As at previous time points children whose fathers were in professional (class I or II non manual) work showed a reduced incidence of 'risk' for Conduct problems, while those whose fathers were absent showed increase 'risk' for Conduct problems and peer problems. Children whose fathers were in semi-skilled manual work were more likely to show emotional symptoms.

Table 1A.23 Father's occupation level and percentage of children identified 'at social/behavioural risk' at the end Year 1

	All children	'at risk' Emotional symptoms	'at risk' Conduct problems	'at risk' Peer problems
Professional I non manual	8.1	6.7	6.3	7.0
Other professional II non manual	19.7	18.2	10.8	16.0
Skilled non man III non manual	12.6	7.6	10.5	11.5
Skilled manual III manual	23.1	21.8	22.3	21.4
Semi skilled IV manual	11.5	15.6	12.0	13.4
Unskilled V manual	2.4	2.7	3.0	3.2
Never worked	0.6	0.9	1.8	0.3
Father absent	20.7	24.4	30.7	27.2
Unknown	1.3	2.2	2.4	0.0
Chi-square	--	ns	$X^2 = 46.571, p<0.001$	ns

• Mother's marital status

The relationship between 'risk' status and marital status remained similar to earlier time points. Significant differences between the groups were found for all three scales. Children coming from single parent families were somewhat over-represented in the 'at risk' categories for Conduct problems and Peer problems, and children coming from families where parents were married, and living together were slightly under-represented, especially for conduct problems.

Table 1A.24 Mother's marital status and percentage of children identified as 'at social/behavioural risk' at the end of Year 1

	All children	'at risk' Emotional symptoms	'at risk' Conduct problems	'at risk' Peer problems
Never married, single parent	13.1	13.8	20.2	16.0
Never married, living with partner	14.2	14.7	14.5	13.1
Married, live with spouse	60.3	55.6	48.8	53.7
Separated/divorced	10.4	10.7	13.9	15.3
Widow/widower	0.2	0.4	0.0	0.3
Other	0.5	2.2	0.0	1.6
Unknown	1.3	2.7	2.7	0.0
Chi-square	--	$x^2 = 15.102$, $p<0.05$	$x^2 = 30.705$, $p<0.001$	$x^2 = 20.985$, $p<0.05$

Home environment characteristics of children 'at risk' on social/behavioural measures

• Overall home learning scale

The relationship between home learning environment and social/behavioural 'risk' was somewhat weaker at the end of Year 1 than was found at pre-school or school entry. Nonetheless, children are more likely to be identified as 'at risk' for Conduct problems in the lowest home learning groups, and less likely in the highest groups[10].

Table 1A.25 Home learning environment and percentage of children identified as 'at social/behavioural risk' at the end of Year 1

	All children	'at risk' Emotional symptoms	'at risk' Conduct problems	'at risk' Peer problems
Mean home learning score	23.7 (sd=7.5)	23.2 (sd=8.0)	21.7 (sd=8.2)	22.7 (sd=7.7)
0-13	8.1	11.1	12.3	10.5
14-19	20.8	24.0	24.7	24.6
20-24	23.7	20.0	24.4	21.1
25-32	32.0	28.9	25.3	31.0
33-45	12.6	13.3	9.3	9.9
Unknown	2.9	2.7	3.9	2.9
Chi-square	--	ns	$x^2 = 20.376$, $p<0.001$	ns

Multiple disadvantage and social/behavioural 'at risk' status at the end Year 1

As at previous time points the links between multiple disadvantage and 'at risk' status for social/behavioural development were investigated for the end of Year 1 assessments. Within the groups of children identified as 'at risk' there was evidence that children experiencing higher levels of disadvantage were more likely to be identified as 'at risk' for Conduct problems and to a lesser extent Peer problems.

---

[10] The correlation between conduct problem score and home learning score =-0.14 (p<0.01)

Table 1A.26 Multiple disadvantage and percentage of children identified as 'at social/behavioural risk' at the end of Year 1

	All children	'at risk' Emotional symptoms	'at risk' Conduct problems	'at risk' Peer problems
Mean MD score	1.7 (sd=1.5)	1.8 (sd=1.5)	2.2 (sd=1.6)	1.9 (sd=1.6)
0	23.7	20.4	15.1	17.9
1-2	47.7	47.1	43.4	48.2
3-4	19.7	23.6	25.6	22.0
5+	4.7	4.4	9.3	7.3
Unknown	4.3	4.4	6.6	4.5
Chi-square	--	ns	$x^2 = 39.621, p<0.001$	$x^2 = 11.914, p<0.05$

Relationships between cognitive and social/behavioural 'at risk' status at the end of Year 1

We investigated whether young children with low cognitive attainments were also identified as having social/behavioural problems in their teacher's assessments at the end of Year 1. Past research has found modest but significant relationships between poor cognitive attainment and behaviour problems (Mortimore et al., 1988; Plomin et al., 2002). The EPPE pre-school sample showed similar patterns of association, the strongest negative correlation found for Hyperactivity, where correlations were -0.32 and -0.37 for the association with Reading and Mathematics assessments respectively. This inverse relationship indicates that children who show more hyperactivity also tend to have poorer attainments at age 6 years plus.

Table 1A.27 Correlations between cognitive and social/behavioural assessments at the end of Year 1

	Pro-social	Hyperactivity	Emotional symptoms	Conduct problems	Peer problems
Primary Reading Test	0.16	-0.32	-0.12	-0.14	-0.11
Mathematics 6	0.21	-0.37	-0.13	-0.20	-0.12

Tables1A.28-1.A.30 below show that a child 'at risk' on either cognitive assessment is more likely to be also 'at risk' for Conduct problems than Emotional symptoms or Peer problems, although only just over quarter of those 'at risk' on cognitive assessments are 'at risk' for Conduct problems.

Table 1A.28 Conduct problems and cognitive 'risk' classifications at the end of Year 1

	'at risk' cognitive	No. and % of overall sample 'at risk' on both	% of 'at risk' on cognitive also 'at risk' on Conduct problems
'at risk' Conduct problems	Reading	67 (2.9%)	26.4%
	Mathematics	89 (3.9%)	28.4%

Table 1A.29 Emotional symptoms and cognitive 'risk' classifications at the end of Year 1

	'at risk' cognitive	No. and % of overall sample 'at risk' on both	% of 'at risk' on cognitive also 'at risk' on emotional symptoms
'at risk' emotional symptoms	Reading	50 (2.1%)	17.1%
	Mathematics	39 (1.7%)	12.5%

Table 1A.30 Peer problems and cognitive 'risk' classifications at the end of Year 1

	'at risk' cognitive	No. and % of overall sample 'at risk' on both	% of those 'at risk' on cognitive also 'at risk' on peer problems
'at risk' peer problems	Reading	61 (2.6%)	21.9%
	Mathematics	67 (2.9%)	21.3%

An index of social/behavioural 'risk' was created from the five Goodman scales. Table 1A.31 below highlights the fact that, from the EYTSEN sample, roughly 70% of children identified as 'at cognitive risk' for either reading or mathematics were also identified as 'at risk' on at least one of the social/behavioural scales. Only a tiny minority, less than one percent of the overall sample, was found to be 'at risk' for all five scales and at least one cognitive outcome.

Table 1A.31 Tabulation of cognitive 'at risk' status and multiple behavioural 'risk'*

	Reading	Mathematics
'at risk' on no behavioural measures	99 (33.9%)	95 (30.4%)
'at risk' any behavioural	64 (21.9%)	79 (25.2%)
'at risk' 2 behavioural	49 (16.8%)	51 (16.3%)
'at risk' 3 behavioural	48 (16.4%)	52 (16.6%)
'at risk' 4 behavioural	20 (6.8%)	28 (8.9%)
'at risk' 5 behavioural	12 (4.1%)	8 (2.6%)
Valid total No 'at risk' (i.e. had behavioural 'at risk' classifications)	292	313

*Percentages of children based on sample 'at risk' for either reading or mathematics.

Table 1A.32 explores this issue in a slightly different way. It focuses on the children in Year 1 not classified as 'at risk' on any social/behavioural scale. In all under 8% of such children were found to be 'at risk' for reading or mathematics. By contrast, if we compare this to children identified as 'at risk' for three or more of the social/behavioural scales, we find that a substantial minority (around 28 to 30%) were also 'at risk' for reading or mathematics.

Table 1A.32 Percentage of children 'at risk' (by behavioural 'risk' category)

	Reading	Mathematics
'at risk' on no behavioural	99 (7.8%)	95 (7.5%)
'at risk' any behavioural	64 (12.6%)	79 (15.7%)
'at risk' 2 behavioural	49 (18.2%)	51 (19.3%)
'at risk' 3 behavioural	48 (28.1%)	52 (30.6%)
'at risk' 4 behavioural	20 (26.3%)	28 (36.8%)
'at risk' 5 behavioural	12 (60.0%)	8 (40.0%)
Valid total No 'at risk' (i.e. had behavioural 'at risk' classifications)	292	313

These results suggest that, for a minority of children in Key Stage 1, there are strong links between social/behavioural problems and very low levels of attainment. Such children can be seen as particularly vulnerable and of special interest in terms of SEN. They may be particularly likely to suffer difficulties due to low self-esteem and motivation and disengagement with school, as they grow older. They are a group of special concern for tackling potential social exclusion. Future follow up will establish whether these children continue to be identified as 'at risk' or are identified as having SEN across KS2.

SECTION 1B: Patterns of progress and changes in young children's cognitive and social/behavioural development across the pre-school period up to the end of Year 1

EYTSEN Technical Paper 1 addressed the issue of changes in children's 'risk' status across the pre-school period, and found that approximately 10% of pupils remained 'at risk' across this period, and could be considered the most vulnerable group. The table below looks at movement across the early years of primary school in 'risk' status.

Table 1B.1 Movement in and out of 'at risk' status from primary entry to end of Year 1 for cognitive and social/behavioural measures[11]

	Out of 'risk'		Into 'risk'		Never 'at risk'		Always 'at risk'	
	N	%	N	%	N	%	N	%
Primary Reading	258	10.7	161	6.7	1842	76.7	141	5.9
Mathematics	255	9.4	178	7.5	1791	75.2	188	7.9
Emotional symptoms	354	15.7	179	7.9	1687	74.7	38	1.7
Conduct problems	246	11.0	176	7.8	1680	74.8	143	6.4
Peer problems	232	10.3	205	9.1	1734	76.6	92	4.1

It can be seen from the table above that around three quarters of children in the main pre-school sample were not identified as 'at risk' at either entry to primary school or the end of Year 1 for either Reading or Mathematics. By contrast, just 5.9% for Reading and 7.9% for Mathematics were classified as 'at risk' (GCA) on both occasions (6.6 per cent were identified as 'at risk' on both occasions for Pre-Reading and 7.0 per cent for Early Number Concepts across the pre-school period). Those identified as 'at risk' at both entry to primary school and again at the end of Year 1 are expected to be more likely to require some form of additional learning support at school and may be identified as having some form of SEN related to learning difficulties. It can also be seen that around 7% of children had moved into 'at risk' status by the end of Year 1 and a slightly larger proportion moved out of 'at risk' status (around 10%) for either Reading or Mathematics.

Movement in 'risk' status across three time points: entry to pre-school, entry to primary school and the end of Year 1

As can be seen in Table 1B.2, the number of children classified as 'at risk' over three time points is much smaller than over the two time points only. Approximately 18-19% of children are identified as 'at risk' on cognitive measures on one time point, nine percent on two time points, but only 3-4% are found to be 'at risk' over three time points. These are young children for whom early intervention and support may be most essential.

---

[11] Movement in 'risk' status from Pre-Reading to Primary Reading, Early number concepts to Mathematics 6, Antisocial/worried/upset to Emotional Symptoms, Antisocial/worried/upset to Conduct problems, Peer sociability to Peer problems.

Table 1B.2 Movement in 'risk' status across three time points: entry to pre-school, entry to primary school and the end of Year 1[12]

	Never 'at risk'		'at risk' one time point		'at risk' two time points		'at risk' three time points	
	N	%	N	%	N	%	N	%
Primary Reading	1632	68.3	456	19.2	219	9.2	63	2.6
Mathematics	1614	68.7	432	18.4	212	9.1	88	3.7
Emotional symptoms	1406	62.7	632	28.2	191	8.5	14	0.6
Conduct problems	1416	63.5	547	24.5	198	8.9	69	3.1
Peer problems	1504	66.8	533	23.7	174	7.7	41	1.8

The proportion of children 'at risk' over three time points for Reading, Mathematics and Conduct problems is fairly similar, whilst only a tiny amount of children are 'at risk' for emotional symptoms over the three time points. The proportion 'at risk' over three time points was also much lower for peer problems. This suggests that SEN in certain areas such as attainment and conduct maybe more firmly rooted from an early age or easier to distinguish.

Table 1B.3 below displays the numbers and percentages of children identified as 'at risk' status at different time points broken down to display the percentage 'at risk' at each permutation of time point. It can be seen that around two thirds of children are not identified as 'at risk' for a particular measure on any occasion (varying from 62.7% for Emotional symptoms to 68.7% for Mathematics). These figures suggest that using assessments for prediction of later need maybe more useful for cognitive measures and conduct/antisocial related assessments. Assessing children at entry to pre-school, a time of important and potentially stressful change in a child's life, maybe less likely to give reliable predictions for areas of social/behaviour such as Emotional symptoms and Peer problems.

Table 1B.3 Trajectories of 'risk' across three time points: entry to pre-school, entry to primary school and the end of Year 1

	Primary Reading		Maths		Emotional symptoms		Conduct problems		Peer problems	
'at risk' at all 3 time points	63	2.6	88	3.7	14	0.6	69	3.1	41	1.8
Not 'at risk' at all 3 time points	1632	68.3	1614	68.7	1406	62.7	1416	63.5	1504	66.8
'at risk' time point 1 only	190	8.0	159	6.8	269	12.0	255	11.4	222	9.9
'at risk' time point 2 only	167	7.0	151	6.4	219	9.8	166	7.4	146	6.5
'at risk' time point 3 only	99	4.2	122	5.2	144	6.4	126	5.7	165	7.3
'at risk' time points 1 & 2	89	3.8	68	2.9	147	6.6	76	3.4	84	3.7
'at risk' time points 1 & 3	56	2.4	54	2.3	34	1.5	49	2.2	39	1.7
'at risk' time points 2 & 3	74	3.1	92	3.9	10	0.4	73	3.3	51	2.3

It must be noted that the use of cut off points to identify those 'at risk' provides a very strict method of identifying those potentially most vulnerable for SEN. Some children might have scores below the cut off on one occasion but just above on another. Thus those scoring below the cut off on two or three occasions over several years are likely to be those with the lowest attainments or showing the greatest behavioural difficulties for an extended period.

---

[12] Movement in 'risk' status from internal GCA to pre-reading to PRT, internal SNC to Early number concepts to Mathematics, Antisocial/worried/upset to Antisocial/worried/upset to Conduct problems, Antisocial/worried/upset to Antisocial/worried/upset to Emotional symptoms, Peer sociability to Peer sociability to Peer problems.

Multiple disadvantage and movement in 'risk' status across three time points

Table 1.B.4 shows patterns of movement in 'at risk' status for the sample in terms of cognitive and social/behavioural development across three time points in relation to multiple disadvantage. The results show that there is a clear difference between the majority of children who comprise the 'never 'at risk' group for Primary Reading, and those who were identified as 'at risk' on three occasions (entry to target pre-school, start of primary school and the end of Year 1). In all 51.7% of those in the 'always 'at risk' group experienced three or more disadvantage factors, compared with only 16.7% of those in the 'never 'at risk' group. Likewise, under 5.5% experienced no disadvantage factors compared with a figure of 30.7% for the never 'at risk' group.

The picture for those moving in and out of 'at risk' status indicates that these were somewhat less disadvantage than the always 'at risk' group, but much more disadvantaged than the 'never 'at risk' group. In all, 42.1% of those who moved in or out of 'at risk' status experienced three or more disadvantage factors.

The results for Mathematics are similar. In all 59.2% of those in the 'always 'at risk' group experienced 3 or more disadvantage factors, compared with only 17.4% of those in the 'never 'at risk' group. Likewise, 6.2% experienced no disadvantage factors compared with a figure of 30.2% for the never 'at risk' group. In all, 49.9% of those who moved in or out of 'at risk' status experienced 3 or more disadvantage factors.

Again these results point to the strong links between multiple disadvantage and cognitive attainment. Ways of combating social disadvantage and promoting the cognitive development of young children most 'at risk' during the early years, and making specific additional support available during the first years at primary school may be necessary to ensure such children do not fall further behind as they move through KS2 and into secondary school.

Table 1B.4 Multiple disadvantage and changes in young children's 'at risk' status over the pre-school period up to the end of Year 1

	Never 'at risk'		'at risk' one time point		'at risk' two time points		'at risk' three time points	
	N	%	N	%	N	%	N	%
Reading								
0	483	30.7	71	16.2	15	7.3	5	5.5
1-2	826	52.6	198	45.2	90	43.7	39	42.9
3-4	228	14.5	134	30.6	76	36.9	36	39.6
5+	35	2.2	35	8.0	25	12.1	11	12.1
Mathematics								
0	471	30.2	72	17.8	18	8.7	5	6.2
1-2	819	52.5	184	45.5	94	45.2	28	34.6
3-4	231	14.8	123	30.4	69	33.2	36	44.4
5+	40	2.6	25	6.2	27	13.0	12	14.8
Emotional symptoms								
0	358	26.3	143	24.0	40	22.1	1	7.7
1-2	678	49.8	304	50.9	82	45.3	9	69.2
3-4	265	19.5	121	20.3	47	26.0	1	7.7
5+	60	4.4	29	4.9	12	6.6	2	15.4
Conduct problems								
0	369	26.9	121	23.2	36	20.0	12	17.9
1-2	687	50.1	260	49.9	96	53.3	25	37.3
3-4	264	19.3	108	20.7	36	20.0	22	32.8
5+	51	3.7	32	6.1	12	6.7	8	11.9
Peer problems								
0	411	28.6	100	19.4	29	17.4	3	7.3
1-2	716	49.7	278	53.9	69	41.3	15	36.6
3-4	262	18.2	108	20.9	47	28.1	18	43.9
5+	48	3.3	30	5.8	22	13.2	5	12.2

A higher proportion of boys remained 'at risk' across the pre-school period up to the end of Year 1 (for Reading, 65% of those 'at risk' over three time points were boys compared to 50% of those not 'at risk' on any time point. For Mathematics, 60% of those 'at risk' over three time points were boys compared to 50% of those not 'at risk' on any time point). Home learning environment showed a particularly strong relationship with staying 'at risk'. Over one third of children with the lowest home learning scores remained 'at risk' across the three time points compared with only 4% of children not 'at risk' at any time points for both Reading and Mathematics.

Type of pre-school provision and change in 'risk' status over three time points

EYTSEN Technical Paper 1 explored young children's movement in and out of 'risk' over the pre-school period for children who had experienced different types of pre-school provision. It is now possible to look at how these children are fairing at the end of Year 1, to assess whether there are still differences in child outcomes between pre-school provision types.

Looking at the change in 'at risk' status for young children from entry to pre-school to entry to the end of Year 1 in primary school, there are differences between types of pre-school providers. Integrated (combined) centres had the lowest percentage of children remaining 'at risk' for all outcomes except mathematics. Only 6% of those originally identified as 'at risk' on general cognitive ability (GCA) were still identified as 'at risk' for reading at entry to primary school and also at the end of Year 1 (see table 1B.5 below).

Private day nurseries had much higher percentages of children who were never 'at risk' than other pre-school types for cognitive outcomes, and integrated centres (which combined care and education) had much lower percentages, reflecting the more advantaged intake demographics of private day nurseries where parents pay for places. Private day nurseries tended to serve more affluent groups while integrated centres are often located in highly disadvantaged areas and target provision for such groups.

Table 1B.5 Proportion of children 'at risk' at entry to the study still 'at risk' at the end of Year 1 (all three time points)

	Reading		Mathematics		Emotional symptoms		Conduct problems		Peer problems	
	N	%	N	%	N	%	N	%	N	%
Nursery Class	16	20.5	24	32.4	12	10.5	2	2.2	11	13.6
Playgroup	16	18.6	17	20.0	20	7.9	4	4.3	7	22.2
Private Day Nursery	7	21.9	7	18.9	8	8.7	1	1.2	4	9.4
Local Authority	13	18.8	11	19.0	19	20.5	4	4.0	9	19.2
Nursery schools	8	9.6	21	25.6	8	10.8	3	4.7	8	12.5
Combined centres	3	6.0	8	24.2	2	7.1	0	0.0	2	8.7

SECTION 1C: Assessing the performance of children with no pre-school experience

By primary school entry children in the pre-school sample had an average attendance of 200 sessions (a session is approx. 2.5 hours or half a day) of pre-school experience, though this average varies significantly by pre-school type (lowest for playgroups, highest for Local Authority Day Nurseries). By definition those in the 'home' sample had little or no experience (more or less than 10 weeks of 2 or fewer sessions a week, equivalent to less than 50 hours). It must be remembered that the children in this sample who did not attend pre-school were demographically different form those who had pre-school experience, which may reflect the picture nationally[13]. Approximately one quarter of the total 'home' sample could not take the Picture Naming, Verbal comprehension and Early Number concepts subscales due to low levels of English. In addition Pre-Reading assessments were available for only 77 % of the total 'home' sample, since these assessments could not be made with validity or reliability for children with little fluency in English. Thus the attainment 'gap' between 'home' and pre-school sample children is likely to reflect a fairly conservative estimate, given that entry to primary school baseline assessments could not be conducted for a substantial proportion of the 'home' sample.

Comparisons of children with and without pre-school experience at entry to primary school

Full details of defining 'at risk' status at entry to primary school are given in EYTSEN Technical Paper 1. Briefly, children were identified as 'at risk' in relation to national and sample norms, for a range of cognitive outcomes including General Cognitive Ability and Pre-Reading and Early Number concepts.

General ability levels, as tested by the BAS II assessments were significantly lower for children with no pre-school experience, than for the pre-school sample. When using nationally standardised scores, the 'home' children scored an average GCA score of 83, more than one standard deviation below the national average of 100. In contrast, on average children with pre-school experience scored 97 for GCA. It must be noted that within each group there was a sizable degree of variation around the mean. Table 1C.1 displays the subscale scores for the two groups of children for nationally standardised scores. For these subscales a national mean of 50 and standard deviation of 10 is the norm.

Table 1C.1 Nationally standardised ability scores for children with and without pre-school experience

	Entry to primary school cognitive assessment scores Nationally standardised BAS subscale scores				
	Pattern construction	Verbal Comp	Picture similarities	Picture naming	Early number Concepts
'Home'	41.4 (sd=12.8)	38.2 (sd=9.4)	46.4 (sd=8.8)	40.5 (sd=10.6)	42.7 (sd=8.6)
'Pre-school'	48.4 (sd=8.7)	45.7 (sd=10.2)	48.7 (sd=10.2)	51.4 (sd=9.3)	48.8 (sd=8.2)
t-test Significance	p<0.001	p<0.001	p<0.001	p<0.001	p<0.001

When the scores were standardised within the EPPE sample, we can see that the 'home' children's average score lay on the 85 cut off for 'at risk' for the EPPE group (average score for pre-school children set to 100). An additional assessment, for which we have internally standardised scores only, was the Pre-Reading assessment. Made up of phonological awareness (alliteration and rhyme) and letter recognition, this measure taps into important early reading skills. The 'home' children also performed significantly below pre-school children for this

---

[13] A higher proportion of these pupils were from ethnic minority groups (see EYTSEN Technical Paper 1).

assessment at entry to primary school ('home' children mean score =43.8, standard deviation= 9.5; pre-school score =50.0, standard deviation= 10.0, p<0.001).

Table 1C.2 Internally standardised BAS scores for children with and without pre-school experience

	Entry to primary school cognitive assessment scores Internally standardised BAS scores				
	Pattern construction	Verbal Comp	Picture similarities	Picture naming	Early number
'home'	44.1 (sd=9.3)	40.6 (sd=10.9)	43.8 (sd=10.3)	41.5 (sd=10.9)	42.4 (sd=9.8)
'Pre-school'	50.0 (sd=10.0)	50.0 (sd=10.0)	50.0 (sd=10.0)	50.0 (sd=10.0)	50.0 (sd=10.0)
t-test Significance	p<0.001	p<0.001	p<0.001	p<0.001	p<0.001

Although the 'home' children scored significantly lower than the EPPE children on all cognitive outcomes, the biggest differences were found for the language measures: Picture Naming and Verbal comprehension (for the internally standardised scores). This may reflect the emphasis on verbal curriculum in the pre-school settings, but also the unavailability of such resources in the 'home' life of EAL children. The smallest difference was found for Picture similarities (a measure of non-verbal reasoning skills).

EYTSEN Technical Paper 1 also provides details of the social/behavioural assessments completed by class teachers when children entered primary school (usually into a reception class). Items from the Adaptive Social Behavioural Inventory (ASBI) were analysed and a number of underlying dimensions covering important aspects of young children's social behaviour identified.

Table 1C.3 Social/behavioural scores for children with and without pre-school experience at entry to primary school

	Entry to primary school behavioural assessment scores					
	Independence & concentration	Co-operation & conformity	Peer sociability	Anti-social/ Worried/ upset	Peer empathy	Confidence
'home'	3.16 (sd=0.89)	3.62 (sd=0.78)	3.12 (sd=0.84)	3.28 (sd=0.63)	3.08 (sd=0.91)	3.36 (sd=0.87)
Preschool	3.56 (sd=0.83)	3.94 (sd=0.68)	3.67 (sd=0.70)	3.26 (sd=0.65)	3.51 (sd=0.78)	3.93 (sd=0.73)
t-test Sig	p<0.001	p<0.001	p<0.001	ns	p<0.001	p<0.001

The 'home' children scored significantly less well than the pre-school sample on all the social/behavioural factors except Anti-social/worried/upset. The largest differences were found for Peer sociability and Confidence. The smallest differences were for Co-operation and conformity and Anti-social/worried/upset.

Table 1C.4 shows the proportion of children in the 'home' sample and those in the pre-school sample identified as 'at risk'. Striking differences emerged, especially for cognitive 'risk' in relation to national norms where over half the 'home' sample were classified as 'at risk', (over twice the proportion of 'home' sample as pre-school sample children identified) and also for Confidence and Peer sociability (nearly three times as many 'home' children identified as 'at risk').

Table 1C.4 Proportion of children with and without pre-school experience identified as 'at risk' at entry to primary school

	Entry to primary school cognitive assessment scores Proportion of children identified 'at risk'			
	General Cognitive Ability (national)	General Cognitive Ability (internal)	Pre-Reading	Early Number
Cut off	85.0	85.0	40.0	40.0
% of 'home' 'at risk'	51.7*	48.3*	40.4	44.9
% of pre-school 'at risk'	21.0	16.2	16.8	17.9

*Calculated for children with 3 or more subscales available

It has already been noted that the 'home' sample, were more socio-economically disadvantaged than the pre-school sample. Proportionately more were from ethnic minority backgrounds and EAL (53.5% of the 'home', but 74.5% of the pre-school sample were of white UK heritage, 38.2% of 'home' compared with 8.7% of pre-school children were EAL). Moreover, a significantly higher proportion, were receiving free school meals (an indicator of low income) (33.9% compared with 22.5%) and had mothers who had no qualifications (57% compared with 18.1%).

Table 1C.5 The Characteristics of 'home' Children Compared with Children who attended a Pre-school Centre

		Children from target pre-schools centres		'home' children	
		n	%	n	%
Gender:	male	1489	52.1	146	46.5
	female	1368	47.9	168	53.5
Ethnicity*	White UK	2127	74.5	168	53.5
	White European	118	4.1	4	1.3
	Black Caribbean	116	4.1	0	0
	Black African	64	2.2	2	0.6
	Black other	22	0.8	0	0
	Indian	55	1.9	12	3.8
	Pakistani	75	2.6	102	32.5
	Bangladeshi	25	0.9	15	4.8
	Chinese	5	0.2	0	0
	Other	62	2.2	4	1.2
	Mixed heritage	185	6.5	7	2.2
English as a Second Language		249	8.7	118	38.2
Receiving free school meals		598	22.5	103	33.9
3 or more siblings		374	13.4	109	39.5
Mother has no formal qualification		501	18.1	146	57.0
Area	East Anglia	559	19.6	91	29.0
	Shire Counties	594	20.8	10	3.2
	Inner London	656	23.0	11	3.5
	North-east	503	17.6	75	23.9
	Midlands	545	19.1	127	40.4

*not known excluded

Analyses for the main EPPE study (reported in EPPE Technical Papers 8a and 8b) have shown, that even taking into account these important differences in background, the 'home' sample are at a cognitive disadvantage in Pre-Reading, Early Number Concepts and Language when starting school. It is concluded that pre-school experience confers a significant positive benefit on cognitive development and on several areas of social behaviour, especially Peer Sociability, at primary school entry.

Due to the strong link between multiple disadvantage, cognitive attainment and 'at risk' status, already identified for the pre-school sample and discussed in earlier sections, it is important to establish whether the 'home' sample are more 'at risk' of SEN than other children across all levels of disadvantage. If so this has important implications for policy makers, practitioners and parents since it would show that pre-school experience can help to reduce the number of children potentially 'at risk' of developing SEN and provide a better start to school for the most vulnerable groups.

Multiple disadvantage and 'at risk' status for children without pre-school experience
A multiple disadvantage measure was calculated comprising child, parent and family factors but not including 'home' learning environment. This allowed the contribution of home learning environment to be identified separately ('home' learning environment details are reported subsequently).

Table 1C.6 Multiple disadvantage indicators used to make up the overall multiple disadvantage index

Child variables	Disadvantage indicator
• English as an Additional language • Large family • Pre-maturity/ low birth weight	English as additional language 3 or more siblings Premature at birth or below 2500 grams
Parent variables	
• Mother's highest qualification level • Social class of Father's occupation • Father's employment status • Young mother • Lone parent • Mother's employment status	No qualifications Semi-skilled, unskilled, never worked, absent father Not employed Age 13-17 at birth of sample child Single parent Not working

When children are matched according to multiple disadvantage levels, a significantly larger proportion of 'home' children were identified as 'at risk' than children who had attended a pre-school centre (table 1C.7). Differences are also evident in the mean scores for the two groups (Table 1C.8).

Table 1C.7 Percentage of children identified as 'at risk' using multiple disadvantage indicators at entry to primary school

Number of factors	Pre-school sample children			'Home' children		
	General cognitive ability	Pre Reading 'risk'	Early number concepts 'risk'	General cognitive ability	Pre Reading 'risk'	Early number concepts 'risk'
0	6.6	7.2	9.4	33.3#	22.2#	22.2#
1-2	13.1	16.8	14.8	35.5	37.5	33.3
3-4	34.5	28.5	34.3	51.0	38.7	45.3
5+	54.7	44.0	55.8	70.8	46.7	69.0
n	2582	2567	2560	185	185	184

Less than 10 pupils
N.B. 'General cognitive ability' refers to 'strong cognitive risk'

Table 1C.8 Children's mean scores in cognitive assessments at entry to primary school using multiple disadvantage indicators

No of factors	Pre-school sample children			'home' children		
	General cognitive ability	Pre-Reading 'risk'	Early number concepts 'risk'	General cognitive ability	Pre-Reading 'risk'	Early number concepts 'risk'
0	106.4 (13.6)	53.3 (9.9)	53.7 (9.1)	97.3 (13.7)	53.0 (13.2)	53.0 (13.2)
1-2	101.0 (13.9)	50.4 (9.6)	50.3 (9.3)	90.9 (14.7)	44.7 (10.4)	44.3 (9.4)
3-4	91.5 (13.8)	45.2 (10.1)	45.2 (8.4)	85.5 (12.8)	43.6 (8.9)	41.4 (8.0)
5+	83.4 (16.7)	40.1 (11.6)	42.2 (9.1)	79.6 (12.4)	41.6 (6.8)	38.3 (10.7)
n	2582	2567	2560	185	185	184

( ) Standard deviation in brackets

A significant number of the 'home' group were EAL (spoke English as an additional language) (EAL). Further analyses were conducted on just this group of children. EAL children had an increased likelihood of being identified as 'at risk' generally, but especially if they hade no pre-school experience. In total, 46% of EAL children with pre-school experience were identified as being 'at risk' for GCA compared with 80% of 'home' children.

Table 1C.9 Mean scores at entry to Primary school – Children for whom English is an additional language

	Pre-school sample			'Home' children		
	General cognitive ability	Pre-Reading 'risk'	Early number concepts 'risk'	General cognitive ability	Pre-Reading 'risk'	Early number concepts 'risk'
Mean scores	87.3 (14.5)	47.8 (8.6)	44.5 (10.1)	78.1 (12.1)	41.8 (8.1)	38.7 (9.8)
% 'at risk'	45.8	38.2	21.4	79.6	50.0	59.2
n	216	201	207	49	48	49

( ) Standard deviation in brackets   N.B. 'General cognitive ability' refers to 'strong cognitive risk'

Even when the EAL children are excluded a marked difference between children of similar multiple disadvantage level, with and without pre-school experience is apparent. This indicates that EAL status is not the only explanation for the attainment gap between 'home' children and those who attended a pre-school centre.

Different combinations of multiple disadvantage were also explored. Table 1C.10 below uses information about three key factors: mother holding no qualifications, father unemployed, and mother unemployed, on which the 'home' and pre-school sample differed. Proportionately more of the 'home' group was 'at risk'. The difference is most marked for General Cognitive Ability scores (GCA) where only 42% of the pre-school, but 68% of the 'home' sample were classified as 'at risk' when they started primary school.

Table 1C.10 Mean scores at entry to Primary school using mother no qualifications and father unemployed, and mother's employment

Number of factors	Pre-school sample children			'Home' children		
	General cognitive ability*	Pre-Reading 'risk'	Early number concepts 'risk'	General cognitive ability	Pre-Reading 'risk'	Early number concepts 'risk'
Mean scores	88.3 (14.1)	44.0 (8.9)	43.5 (10.1)	81.0 (12.7)	43.1 (6.8)	41.2 (11.5)
% 'at risk'	41.9	31.1	41.6	68.0	40.0	56.0
n	93	90	89	25	25	25

( ) Standard deviation in brackets   N.B. 'General cognitive ability' refers to 'strong cognitive risk'

Another indicator of special interest is that of low family income, measured by receipt of Free School Meals (FSM). Using this as a comparison it can be seen that more of the 'home' group than those who had attended a pre-school centre were 'at risk' in terms of low cognitive scores when they entered primary school.

Table 1C.11 Mean scores at entry to Primary school for Children in receipt of Free School Meals

Number of factors	Pre-school sample			'Home' children		
	General cognitive ability	Pre-Reading 'risk'	Early number concepts 'risk'	General cognitive ability	Pre-Reading 'risk'	Early number concepts 'risk'
Mean scores	92.4 (14.3)	45.7 (8.9)	45.7 (10.2)	84.4 (13.8)	42.7 (8.3)	42.6 (10.2)
% 'at risk'	31.8	28.4	31.8	53.6	39.3	46.4
n	594	587	592	84	84	84

( ) Standard deviation in brackets
'General cognitive ability' refers to strong

In EYTSEN Technical Paper 1 and earlier in Section 1A of the current paper attention was drawn to the link between the home learning environment and children's 'at risk' status. In order to establish whether differences in the quality of the home learning environment between those who did or did not attend pre-school help to explain the higher proportions identified as 'at risk' for the 'home' sample, further analyses were conducted. These comparisons show that children with similar levels of home learning environment were two to three times more likely to be identified as 'at risk' if they had not attended pre-school.

Table 1C.12 Children 'at risk' at entry to Primary school – levels of Home learning for 'risk' groups

Home learning environment	Pre-school sample			'home' children		
	General cognitive ability 'risk'	Pre-Reading 'risk'	Early number concepts 'risk'	General cognitive ability 'risk'	Pre-Reading 'risk'	Early number concepts 'risk'
0-13	46.8	39.0	45.7	76.9	64.0	65.4
14-19	23.3	21.5	24.0	49.1	43.9	56.1
20-24	13.2	16.9	14.5	39.6	31.3	31.3
25-32	9.9	11.6	13.2	35.0	33.0	36.8
33-45	3.6	6.4	5.2	0.0*	0.0*	9.1*

( ) Standard deviation in brackets
* Only 11 'home' children were in the highest HLE group so this statistic shown should be treated with caution
N.B. 'General cognitive ability' refers to 'strong cognitive risk'

Comparisons of children with and without pre-school experience at the end of Year 1

By the end of Year 1 the 'home' children are still performing significantly below the main EPPE sample for all cognitive outcomes. For social/behavioural outcomes they also perform significantly lower than the main EPPE sample for all outcomes except Conduct problems. This reflects earlier findings at entry to reception.

Table 1C.13 End of Year 1 assessments for children with and without pre-school experience

	Year 1 cognitive assessment scores	
	Primary Reading	**Mathematics**
'Home' children	88.9 (sd=13.4)	91.0 (sd=15.0)
'Pre-school' children	97.2 (sd=15.5)	100.4 (sd=15.1)
t-test Significance	t=8.493, p<0.001	t=9.635, p<0.001

	Year 1 behavioural assessment scores				
	Pro-social	**Hyperactivity**	**Emotional symptoms**	**Conduct problems**	**Peer problems**
'Home' children	6.7 (sd=2.4)	3.7 (sd=2.8)	2.2 (sd=2.2)	1.0 (sd=1.7)	1.9 (sd=1.9)
'Pre-school' children	7.4 (sd=2.4)	3.3 (sd=3.0)	1.5 (sd=2.0)	1.0 (sd=1.6)	1.4 (sd=1.7)
t-test Significance	t=3.256, p<0.001	t=-2.450, p<0.05	t=-5.011, p<0.001	ns	t=-5.182, p<0.001

N.B. High scores in hyperactivity, emotional symptoms, Conduct problems and peer problems represent more negative symptoms

'Home' children were still roughly twice as likely to be identified as 'at risk' at the end of Year 1 for Mathematics and Reading. Smaller differences were found for the social/behavioural assessments, except for Emotional symptoms, where a higher proportion of 'home' children were identified as 'at risk'.

Table 1C.14 Proportion of 'home' and Pre-school children identified as 'at risk' at the end of Year 1

	End of Year 1 cognitive assessment scores Proportion of children identified 'at risk'			
	Primary Reading (national mean)	**Mathematics**	**Primary Reading (sample mean)**	**Mathematics**
Cut off score	85.0	85.0	82.0	85.0
% of 'home' 'at risk'	43.8	36.9	27.6	36.9
% of pre-school 'at risk'	22.7	15.6	12.9	15.6

	End of Year 1 behavioural assessment scores Proportion of children identified 'at risk'				
	Pro-social	**Hyperactivity**	**Emotional symptoms**	**Conduct problems**	**Peer problems**
Cut off score	12.0	6.0	5.0	3.0	4.0
% of 'home' 'at risk'	30.5	26.9	15.1	16.2	17.6
% of pre-school 'at risk'	25.1	23.3	9.4	14.0	13.1

N.B Internal means used to determine the cut off score have been calculated excluding the 'home'

These results indicate that as a group, 'home' children remain at greater 'risk' of SEN during reception and to the end of Year 1. The absence of pre-school experience can be seen as an additional 'risk' factor which acts independently of those child, family and home learning environment characteristics described earlier as associated with 'at risk' status. For multiply disadvantaged young children, missing out on such pre-school experience may be particularly disadvantageous for cognitive development and for other important aspects of social/behavioural development that may help ease the transition to primary school, particularly Peer sociability.

Comparisons of children with and without pre-school experience within a contextualised multilevel model controlling for pupil background

As noted above, the children not attending pre-school were demographically different from the main sample of children. Further analyses were therefore conducted based on the whole sample, rather than focussing only on the 'at risk' group. Statistical models can be used to examine the impact of different factors as predictor's of children's attainments, in this way the net impact of individual measures (e.g. gender, EAL status etc) can be ascertained. The net influence of attending a pre-school can thus be established, taking account of the influence of other important child, family and home learning environment influences. A contextualised multilevel model was run at two time points: entry to primary school and at the end of Year 1. The models sought to explain (statistically) the variation in children's scores on specific attainment measures. The data collected from parents on the first parent interview when children entered the study was used to control for any differences in child, parent and home environment background characteristics between the two groups (pre-school sample and 'home' sample). In this way, we can see if children not attending pre-school had significantly lower attainments than those who had attended pre-school, having taken into account the important differences in background characteristics. Table 1C.15 shows that children without pre-school experience had significantly lower attainments than other children for four out of the five assessments.

Table 1C.15 Multilevel results showing the effect of no pre-school provision at primary school entry

	Pre-Reading	Early number concepts	Language	Peer Sociability	Anti-social / Worried
No pre-school centre provision	-2.685* (0.943)	-1.999* (0.425)	-2.541* (0.526)	-0.359* (0.058)	-0.061 (0.056)

* statistically significant at 0.05 level

It is also of interest to examine the impact on children's cognitive attainment of no pre-school provision compared to the different types of pre-school provision. Thus, type of pre-school was added to the model with no pre-school provision as the comparison group. The results suggest that all types of pre-school provision compared to none show benefits for some outcomes with higher cognitive attainment in early number concepts and language.[14] Table 1C.16 reports the types of pre-school provision showing a positive, statistically significant (at the 0.05 level) impact on attainment. Results of spatial awareness/reasoning are omitted as no significant differences between types of provision were found in the multilevel analysis. For both Language and Early Numbers attainment and Peer Sociability all types show significantly positive effects.

Table 1C.16 Multilevel results showing the effect of no pre-school provision compared to different types of pre-school provision on attainment at primary school entry

	Pre-Reading	Early number concepts	Language	Non-verbal reasoning	Peer Sociability	Anti-social / Worried
Nursery classes	positive	positive	positive		positive	
Playgroups		positive	positive		positive	
Private day	positive	positive	positive	positive	positive	
LA day care	positive	positive	positive	positive	positive	positive (worse)
Nursery schools		positive	positive		positive	
Integrated centres		positive	positive	positive	positive	

Positive = statistically significant at 0.05 level

---

[14] It should be noted that these models could not include pre-school centre intake compositional measures (% mothers with degrees or above) which are particularly relevant to the impact of private day nurseries (see Section 4), because they did not apply to the 'home' group. However, mother's qualification level was controlled for at the child level.

Equivalent analyses were conducted for the child sample at the end of Year 1 to establish whether the 'home' samples' cognitive and social/behavioural development remained behind that of children in the pre-school sample.

Table 1C.17 Multilevel results showing the effect of no pre-school provision at the end of Year 1

	Primary Reading	Mathematics	Emotional symptoms	Conduct problems	Peer problems
No pre-school centre provision	-3.357* (1.254)	-4.480* (1.230)	-0.406* (0.155)	0.242 (0.131)	0.243 (0.150)

* statistically significant at 0.05 level

Table 1C.18 Multilevel results showing the effect of no pre-school provision compared to different types of pre-school provision at the end of Year 1

	Primary Reading	Mathematics	Emotional symptoms	Conduct problems	Peer problems
Nursery classes		positive			
Playgroups		positive	positive		
Private day		positive	positive	negative	
LA day care		positive		negative	
Nursery schools	positive	positive	positive		
Integrated centres	positive				positive

Positive = statistically significant at 0.05 level

It can be seen that having attended a pre-school still confers a significant advantage, particularly in relation to Mathematics and a reduction in emotional problems. Interestingly, however, the 'home' sample were somewhat less likely to show Conduct problems in Year 1 (based on teachers' assessments) than those who had attended private day or Local Authority day nurseries. For Peer problems sociability, the differences were only significant in comparison with those who had attended Integrated centres, while for Reading children who had attended nursery schools or Integrated centres showed significantly higher attainments than the 'home' sample.

These results indicate that pre-school influences continue to affect both cognitive and social/behavioural outcomes across Key Stage 1.

Section 1.D: Teacher Identification of Special Educational Needs

Information about whether a child in the pre-school or 'home' samples had been identified as having any SEN was collected in Year 2 for all children. In addition due to particular interest in this topic for the EYTSEN study, additional data were collected for later cohorts in the study at the end of Year 1. It is of particular interest to establish, which children were identified by their teachers and how this relates to young children's 'at risk' status in terms of measured cognitive or social/behavioural outcomes. Are there some children categorised as 'at risk' by the EYTSEN criteria, who are not identified as having a SEN at school? If so, is this because their needs are not recognised in school, or because only some combinations of possible need are seen to constitute a SEN in school, or to require intervention? Given the link between multiple disadvantage and 'at risk' status revealed in analyses in EYTSEN Technical Paper 1, are multiply disadvantaged children with equivalent low levels of prior attainment (in terms of the 'at risk' cut offs) more or less likely to be identified at school as having any SEN?

Children identified as having SEN during KS1

Table 1.D.1 indicates that just over a quarter of children had been identified as showing some form of SEN during KS1. This is slightly higher than national statistics, which report around 20% of children in nursery and primary schools as having a special educational need in 2002 and approximately 18% in 2003 (DfES, 2002; DfES, 2003). The higher numbers may reflect the somewhat higher incidence of disadvantage amongst the EPPE sample as a whole. Only a very small percentage (2.3%) had a full statement[15]. Most children identified as having SEN received small group or individual support in school in their own class (22% of the total sample). The data reveal that for most types of identification, children without pre-school experience (the 'home' sample) had significantly higher levels of SEN or help reported. This suggests that 'home' children may be particularly vulnerable, and require extra monitoring and support when they begin school.

Table 1D.1 Children identified at school as having any SEN in during Key Stage 1

	Pre-school children		'home' children		All children	
	%	n	%	n	%	n
Child ever recognised as having SEN	25.5	610	42.3	121	27.3	731
Teachers mentions specific Need now	25.3	614	36.9	106	26.5	72
Any provision for SEN given:	27.3	657	41.1	118	28.7	775
SEN within school	19.1	458	32.9	93	20.5	551
Small group/individual support	20.0	481	33.8	96	21.5	577
Special teacher some time	6.6	158	12.7	36	7.2	194
Special class inside school	9.6	230	17.6	50	10.4	280
Special class outside school	0.8	19	0.4	1	0.7	20
SEN met in other ways	1.8	43	2.1	6	1.9	49
Code Of Practice full statement	2.0	49	4.3	12	2.3	61

The relationship between teachers reporting a child had been identified at school as having some form of SEN at the end of Year 1 and the child's attainments in Reading and Mathematics at the end of Year 1 was explored. In particular, comparisons are made with those identified as most 'at risk' of SEN on the basis of low cognitive scores (1+ sd below the sample mean) using the EYTSEN classification. The results reveal that, of those identified as 'at risk' in terms of low scores on the standardised cognitive assessments, over two thirds were reported by teachers as having a SEN or were receiving help for a SEN. In addition, of those not identified as 'at risk'

---

[15] Because this data was collected before the introduction of the present code of practice, all references to code of practice relate to the old code.

using the EYTSEN classification of low cognitive attainment, around 9-12% were identified by teachers as having some SEN or were being monitored for SEN by teachers.

Table 1D.2 Proportion of 'at risk' children for attainment in Year 1 identified by teachers as exhibiting SEN at the end of Year 1 – all children

	Reading		Mathematics		Either Reading or Mathematics 'risk'	
	%	n	%	n	%	n
Any help given or teacher identified a specific SEN	72.9	266	69.7	313	66.8	395
Child ever recognised as having SEN	68.1	245	63.9	283	60.5	352
Teachers mentions specific Need	62.4	227	61.9	278	56.6	334
Code of practice:						
Code Of Practice - statement	3.7	13	3.1	13	2.5	14
Code Of Practice –undergoing statement	3.7	13	3.1	13	2.3	13
Code Of Practice- being considered*	54.2	188	52.5	224	50.0	280
Any type of help for SEN:	68.7	250	65.2	294	62.8	370
SEN within school	56.6	206	52.8	236	49.7	293
Small group/individual support	56.6	206	53.2	238	50.6	298
Special teacher some time	22.5	82	19.7	88	19.5	115
Special class inside school	29.9	109	27.1	121	25.8	152
Learning difficulties and 'risk'						
Monitoring	11.2	36	14.0	57	12.3	66
Now	38.4	124	36.5	150	31.8	171
Reading difficulties and Primary Reading 'risk'						
Monitoring	9.0	29	10.8	44	10.4	56
Now	47.7	154	41.9	171	39.0	209
Number work difficulties and Primary Reading 'risk'						
Monitoring	9.6	31	11.5	47	10.8	58
Now	40.9	132	38.0	155	34.1	183

* stages 1-3 of the COP

Of the children identified as 'at risk' in terms of low scores on the social/behavioural assessments in the EYTSEN study, approximately half were independently reported by teachers as having a SEN or were receiving help for a SEN in Year 1, usually monitored by the Code of Practice (CoP). The agreement between EYTSEN of 'at risk' and teacher identification of SEN was stronger for cognitive than for social/behavioural outcomes. Table 1D:3 gives details.

Table 1D.3 Proportion of 'at risk' children for social/behavioural outcomes identified by teachers as exhibiting SEN at the end of Year 1 – all children

	Emotional symptoms 'risk' %	n	Conduct problems 'risk' %	n	Peer problems 'risk' %	n	Any behavioural 'risk' %	n
Any help given or teacher identified a specific SEN	52.9	137	59.5	213	57.6	144	52.7	380
Child ever recognised as having SEN	44.7	114	52.2	185	46.9	161	43.9	314
Teachers mentions specific Need	43.2	112	51.7	181	48.7	165	43.9	316
Code of practice:								
Code Of Practice statement	2.8	7	3.3	11	3.8	13	2.6	18
Code Of Practice –undergoing statement	0.8	2	2.4	8	3.0	10	1.7	12
Code Of Practice- being considered	37.3	92	40.9	137	35.5	120	34.9	244
Any type of help for SEN:	46.3	120	50.6	179	47.1	161	44.0	317
SEN within school	35.8	92	41.1	145	37.1	125	34.7	247
Small group/individual support	31.4	81	38.8	137	34.7	117	33.0	235
Special teacher some time	14.4	37	11.9	42	13.6	46	11.9	85
Special class inside school	18.6	48	19.3	68	17.2	58	16.8	120
Emotional & behavioural difficulties								
Monitoring	4.3	10	7.7	25	6.1	19	6.1	40
Now	16.6	43	31.4	111	21.8	75	19.9	144
Developmental delay								
Monitoring	2.6	6	3.1	10	2.9	9	1.8	12
Now	4.6	12	3.1	11	5.2	18	3.7	27

* stages 1-3 of the COP

Those children not identified by teachers as receiving help or having any specific SEN, but who were identified by the EYTSEN 'at risk' classification, had significantly higher Reading and Mathematics scores than those identified by teachers. However, the mean scores for those 'at risk' children not identified as having SEN by their teachers were still well below the cut off level (mean score of 74.1 for Reading, and 76.7 for Mathematics). This suggests that some teachers maybe using a more stringent indicator of 'need' than that adopted by the EYTSEN classification (the cut off was 1 sd below the sample mean, thus identifying around 16-17% of the sample).

It is also relevant to establish to what extent teachers reported a child had a SEN amongst children who were not identified by the EYTSEN classification. Overall, quite sizeable numbers of children were identified by teachers but not by the EYTSEN classification (536 children for Reading, 489 for Mathematics). The average score of children identified by teachers but not by the EYTSEN study was found to be very near the sample average (for Reading 99.3 and for Mathematics, 99.8), it appears that such children were not low scoring children.

Of those identified by teachers but not by EYTSEN cognitive classifications, 39% were reported to have a behavioural 'risk'. Nonetheless, the areas of need identified most commonly by teachers for this group were Reading difficulties (29%), Number difficulties (20%), Emotional problems (21%), Learning difficulties (17%) and Medical conditions (11%).

An index of 'need' was created by adding together the number of different specific 'needs' that had been identified by the child's teacher for each child in the sample. The results show that children identified as 'at cognitive risk' by the EYTSEN definition were much more likely to have multiple needs identified by their teachers than those not 'at risk' (see Table 1D.4). The percentage of children recorded by teachers as having one need only is just over one in ten of the sample (11.1% or 277 children). Another ten per cent of the sample was recorded as having

3 or more different needs. Table 1D.4 gives details for all children and for those classified as 'at risk'.

Table 1D.4 Number of teacher identified Special Educational Needs for 'at risk' children in terms of cognitive attainment end of Year1

Number of specific 'needs' identified by teacher	All children*		Reading 'risk'		Mathematics 'risk'		Either Reading or Mathematics 'risk'	
	%	n	%	n	%	n	%	n
0	73.8	1841	37.5	120	38.5	156	43.4	231
1-2	16.1	402	24.4	78	27.7	112	26.1	139
3-4	7.3	183	24.7	79	22.5	91	21.4	114
5+	2.8	70	13.4	43	11.4	46	9.0	48

* not including cohort 1 as not all questions asked

These data suggest that some children with very low attainments (as identified by the EYTSEN research classification) may not be recognized as having a special need in school.

Table 1D.5 presents the results for the analysis of number of needs reported by teachers, in this case for children identified as 'at risk' on different areas of social behaviour. It can be seen that the relationships are less strong than for the cognitive 'at risk' classification. Overall, more children identified as 'at risk' for Conduct problems were reported by teachers as showing a need, and rather fewer for those identified as 'at risk' for Emotional symptoms.

Table 1D.5 Number of teacher identified Special Educational Needs for 'at risk' children (social/behavioural)

No of specific 'needs' Identified by teacher	All children*		Emotional symptoms 'risk'		Conduct problems 'risk'		Peer problems 'risk'		Any behavioural 'risk'	
	%	n	%	n	%	n	%	n	%	n
0	73.9	1841	58.2	153	50.6	164	52.3	158	57.3	373
1-2	16.2	402	23.3	54	27.2	88	25.5	77	24.1	157
3-4	7.3	83	12.1	28	14.2	46	12.6	38	12.0	78
5+	2.8	70	6.5	15	8.0	26	9.6	29	6.6	43

* not including cohort 1 as not all questions asked

Table 1D.6 illustrates the relationship between the number of needs identified by teachers and whether a child was identified as 'at risk' for any cognitive or social/behavioural outcome at the end of Year1.

Table 1D.6 Number of teacher identified Special Educational Needs for 'at risk' children (any EYTSEN 'risk' classification)

No of specific 'needs' Identified by teacher	All children*		Any EYTSEN risk (cognitive or behavioural)	
	%	n	%	n
0	73.1	1841	55.4	544
1-2	16.3	402	24.2	238
3-4	7.3	83	14.5	142
5+	2.8	70	5.9	58

* not including cohort 1 as not all questions asked

The following table (Table 1D.7) indicates which types of SEN were reported by teachers and the numbers of children in the sample (including both the pre-school and 'home' groups) identified for each area of difficulty. It should be noted that children might be classified as experiencing more than one kind of difficulty. The figures indicate that learning/Reading/number and language difficulties were much more likely to be reported than social/behavioural problems for this age group. The results also show that 'home' children were particularly likely to be identified as having a reading or learning difficulty in comparison with those who had attended pre-school.

Table 1D.7 Types of SEN identified by teachers at the end of Years 1 and 2

	Pre-school children		'Home' children		All children	
	%	n	%	n	%	n
Teachers mentions specific Need now	25.3	614	36.9	106	26.5	720
Learning difficulty						
Monitoring	4.2	94	6.0	15	4.3	109
Now	9.3	211	23.2	60	10.8	271
Past	3.1	69	4.6	12	3.2	81
Reading difficulty						
Monitoring	4.8	109	6.4	16	5.0	125
Now	6.4	294	27.1	68	14.4	362
Past	4.6	103	8.0	20	4.9	123
Number difficulty						
Monitoring	4.5	101	6.4	16	4.7	117
Now	10.8	245	21.5	54	11.9	299
Past	3.0	68	5.6	14	3.3	82
Speech and language difficulty						
Monitoring	2.7	61	5.6	14	3.0	175
Now	6.8	163	11.2	32	7.2	195
Past	3.3	79	4.6	13	3.4	92
Emotional & behavioural diff.						
Monitoring	3.0	68	4.4	11	3.1	79
Now	7.5	180	6.3	18	7.3	198
Past	2.8	67	2.1	6	2.7	73
Hearing impairment						
Monitoring	1.3	30	1.6	4	1.4	34
Now	1.0	25	1.4	4	1.1	29
Past	0.7	18	0.7	2	2.7	20
Visual impairment						
Monitoring	0.7	15	0.4	1	0.6	16
Now	1.9	45	4.6	13	2.2	58
Past	0.6	14	0.7	2	0.6	16
Physical impairment						
Monitoring	0.5	12	0.0	0	0.5	12
Now	0.8	19	0.0	0	0.8	19
Past	0.2	5	0.7	2	0.3	7
Medical condition						
Monitoring	0.9	20	0.8	2	0.9	22
Now	3.2	76	5.3	15	3.4	91
Past	0.5	11	1.8	5	0.6	16
Developmental delay						
Monitoring	0.8	19	3.2	8	1.1	27
Now	1.7	41	3.2	9	1.9	50
Past	0.7	19	0.4	1	0.7	20

* Cohort 1 not asked all of these specific questions

Characteristics of children identified by teachers as having a 'need'

The characteristics (child, family and home learning environment) of children identified by teachers as showing either a specific 'need' or as receiving help for a specific 'need' were compared with those of children as a whole to establish whether some groups were over-represented. The results indicate that more children identified by teachers as having a SEN were boys and EAL. The findings were very similar to those reported for the EYTSEN 'at risk' classifications. Again this suggests that the 'at risk' definition and school identification procedures are likely to pick up similar 'types' of children.

Table 1D.8 Gender and percentage of children identified by teachers as having an SEN at end of Year 1

	All children	Teacher identified %	n
Male	52.2	61.4	570
Female	47.8	38.4	359
Chi-sqaure		X^2 = 60.431, p<0.001	

Table 1D.9 Child's language and percentage of children identified by teachers as having an SEN at end of Year 1

	All children	Teacher identified %	n
English	92.5	87.7	808
English not 1st language	7.5	12.8	119
Chi-sqaure		X^2 = 6.116, p<0.05	

Children identified by teachers as having SEN are significantly more likely to have mothers with no qualifications; again the proportions are in line with findings for the EYTSEN 'at risk' classifications.

Table 1D.10 Mother's qualification and percentage of children identified by teachers as having an SEN at end of Year 1

	All children	Teacher identified %	n
None	17.7	28.0	260
16yr vocational	2.0	1.7	16
16 academic	37.5	35.5	330
18 vocational	12.8	11.9	111
18 academic	8.6	7.4	69
Degree or equivalent	13.1	6.9	64
Higher degree	4.7	2.4	22
Other professional	0.7	0.4	4
Other miscellaneous	0.7	0.1	1
Unknown	2.2	5.7	53
Chi-sqaure		X^2 = 88.618, p<0.001	

As with findings for those identified as 'at risk' by the EYTSEN criteria, the analysis shows that children identified by teachers as having a SEN had significantly poorer home learning environment scores. This suggests that, as a group, such children's parents were less likely to engage in activities with their child such as teaching songs and nursery rhymes, reading, painting and drawing, teaching letters and numbers etc.

Table 1D.10 'home' learning environment and percentage of children identified by teachers as having an SEN at the end of Year 1

	All children	Teacher identified	
		%	n
Mean 'home' learning score	23.6 (sd=7.5)	21.3 (sd=7.7)	
0-13	8.4	13.9	129
14-19	20.9	26.0	242
20-24	23.6	21.7	202
25-32	31.9	26.0	242
33-45	12.4	6.9	64
Unknown	2.9	5.5	51
Chi-sqaure		$X^2 = 93.641$, p<0.001	

When multiple disadvantage is considered the results indicate that children identified as having a SEN were significantly more disadvantaged, scoring more highly on the multiple disadvantage index. For example, proportionately more than twice as many children identified as having the highest levels of disadvantage (5+ factors) were identified by teachers as having an SEN than was the case for children as a whole. Again this finding is in accord with that found for the identification of cognitive 'at risk' status using the EYTSEN classification.

Table 1D.11 Multiple disadvantage and percentage of children identified by teachers as having an SEN at end of Year 1

	All children	Teacher identified	
		%	n
Mean MD score	1.7 (sd=1.5)	12.3 (sd=1.7)	
0	23.7	14.2	139
1-2	47.4	42.1	363
3-4	19.8	30.1	238
5+	4.8	11.5	107
Unknown	4.3	9.5	88
Chi-sqaure		$X^2 = 110.412$, p<0.001	

Children young for their year

The EYTSEN definition of children 'at risk' of SEN in terms of low cognitive attainment used age standardized scores because of the known link between age and cognitive development (discussed in EYTSEN Technical Paper 1).

In pre-school and school however it is not always the case that the influence of age is considered in assessing children's work. Previous research has indicated that junior age children young for their year (summer born children) tend to be judged as lower ability by their class teachers (see Mortimore et al, 1988). In addition class teachers rated more summer born children as having behaviour problems.

It is important to establish whether children identified at primary school as having some form of SEN are more likely to be young for their year. If this is the case, the results would suggest that current systems of identification do not adequately acknowledge the influence of age on children's attainment, learning and behaviour.

The EYTSEN research indicates that significantly more summer born (young for their year) children were identified as having a SEN during KS1 and significantly fewer autumn born children (those who are the oldest in the year group).

These findings clearly demonstrate that the systems for identifying SEN used by schools do not adequately acknowledge the impact of age. It may be that because teachers make little use of standardised assessments for this age group that the importance of developmental age is missed when teachers consider children's attainment, learning and behaviour.

The findings suggest that the current emphasis on teacher assessment/judgement may be disadvantageous to summer born children and some may be mistakenly viewed as having SEN because of this.

Ways to ensure that primary school teachers are fully aware of the important implications of pupil age when assessing children, especially in relation to SEN should be given a high priority and appropriate guidance provided for SENCOs. The wider use of standardized assessments may be needed to ensure that sufficient consideration of age effects is made.

Table 1D.12 Term of birth and percentage of children identified by teachers as having an SEN at the end of Year 1

Pre-school and 'Home' sample

	Autumn	Spring	Summer
Has the child ever been recognised as having a SEN?	20.8%	27.5%	33.7%
Any type of SEN mentioned by teacher	20.7%	28.2%	30.7%

Pre-school children only

	Autumn	Spring	Summer
Has the child ever been recognised as having a SEN?	20.0%	24.9%	32.2%
Any type of SEN mentioned by teacher	20.1%	26.4%	29.7%

'Home' children only

	Autumn	Spring	Summer
Has the child ever been recognised as having a SEN?	30.0%	50.5%	43.1%
Any type of SEN mentioned by teacher	27.5%	44.0%	36.4%

Section 2 - The continuing impact of pre-school quality on 'risk' status up to the end of Year 1

In this section the relationship between pre-school centre quality characteristics and the subsequent progress of different 'at risk' groups at the end of Year 1 is examined.

Distribution of 'at risk' children across pre-school settings

Children who had attended integrated (combined) centres still have the highest proportion of children 'at risk' for Mathematics attainment and private day nurseries the lowest proportion. However, the proportion of children classified as 'at risk' who had attended an integrated centre dropped substantially from the start of pre-school to the end of Year 1. It must be remembered that integrated centres catered for much higher numbers of disadvantaged children (reported in EYTSEN technical Paper 1), but that over the pre-school period this form of provision saw proportionately more children making cognitive gains and moving out of 'at risk' status, particularly in relation to promoting better Pre-reading skills. The results suggest that the positive pre-school impact remains evident at the end of Year 1.

Table 2A.1 Distribution of 'at risk' children across pre-school settings

Proportion of children 'at risk' for primary Reading at the end of Year 1											
Nursery class		Playgroup		Private day nursery		Local Authority		Nursery school		Combined	
%	n	%	n	%	n	%	n	%	n	%	n
19.2	104	10.9	55	6.8	30	14.0	51	11.6	51	16.8	23
Proportion of children 'at risk' for primary Mathematics at the end of Year 1											
Nursery class		Playgroup		Private day nursery		Local Authority		Nursery school		Combined	
%	n	%	n	%	n	%	n	%	n	%	n
20.2	109	13.9	69	8.1	35	15.6	56	16.5	72	24.8	34
Proportion of children 'at risk' for primary Emotional symptoms at the end of Year 1											
Nursery class		Playgroup		Private day nursery		Local Authority		Nursery school		Combined	
%	n	%	n	%	n	%	n	%	n	%	n
10.4	54	8.7	44	6.0	26	11.3	40	9.1	40	15.4	21
Proportion of children 'at risk' for primary Conduct problems at the end of Year 1											
Nursery class		Playgroup		Private day nursery		Local Authority		Nursery school		Combined	
%	n	%	n	%	n	%	n	%	n	%	n
12.6	65	12.9	64	10.8	47	23.8	84	12.3	54	13.2	18
Proportion of children 'at risk' for primary Peer problems at the end of Year 1											
Nursery class		Playgroup		Private day nursery		Local Authority		Nursery school		Combined	
%	n	%	n	%	n	%	n	%	n	%	n
11.8	61	13.2	67	13.4	58	18.0	64	11.4	50	9.6	13

Quality in pre-school settings and Special Educational Needs

Details of the information used to create 'centre profiles' for each individual pre-school setting in the study can be found in EYTSEN Technical Paper 1 and EPPE Technical Paper 6. Three measures of centre quality were utilised: The Early Childhood Environment Rating Scale: Revised (ECERS-R, Harms, Clifford and Cryer, 1998), along with an extension of that based on the Desirable Learning Outcomes (ECERS-E, Sylva, Siraj-Blatchford, and Taggart, 2003) and the Caregivers Interaction Scale (CIS, Arnett, 1989) addressing more specifically the interactions between caregivers and children.

The relationship between 'quality' of pre-school and movement in 'risk' status over three time points

The EYTSEN research sought to establish whether children moving out of 'risk' and staying out of 'risk' up to the end of Year 1 attended higher quality pre-school settings than other children. The evidence from the EYTSEN project suggests that this is the case for cognitive outcomes, but not for social/behavioural outcomes at earlier time points (entry to study at 3 years plus and entry to school at rising 5 years). Children who have moved out of 'cognitive risk' by the end of pre-school had attended higher quality pre-school centres when looking at overall cognitive skills (GCA) and Pre-reading. For Early number concepts at entry to primary school, centre quality ratings were also higher for children moving out of 'at risk' status, although differences do not reach statistical significance.

The strongest relationship between quality aspects of pre-schools and 'risk' status over three time points were found for reading and Conduct problems. Children who were always 'at risk' for the Reading outcome (or related outcomes at earlier time points) attended centres with higher observed levels of 'punitiveness' and 'detachment' (measured by the CIS instrument) and lower ECERS-R scores (related to quality of care). Children with Peer problems over three time points were found to come from pre-school centres with higher levels of 'detachment' between children and staff. It appears that children always 'at risk' for Conduct problems (3 time points) attended pre-school settings with higher levels of observed 'detachment' and lower levels of 'positive relationships' between staff and children.

Table 2A.3 Mean scores on quality of pre-school centre and children's levels of 'risk' across three time points for cognitive outcomes

Reading	'at risk' only at entry to the study	'at risk' two time points	Always 'at risk'	Anova[16]
ECERS-R	4.67 (1.05)	4.75 (1.01)	4.27 (1.08)	p<0.01
ECERS-E	ns	ns	ns	ns
CIS				
Positive relationship	ns	ns	ns	ns
Punitiveness	1.41 (0.23)	1.47 (0.26)	1.54 (0.30)	p<0.01
Permissiveness	ns	ns	ns	ns
Detachment	1.33 (0.47)	1.45 (0.50)	1.49 (0.60)	p<0.05
Mathematics	'at risk' only at entry to the study	'at risk' two time points	Always 'at risk'	Anova
ECERS R	ns	ns	ns	ns
ECERS E	ns	ns	ns	ns
CIS				
Positive relationship	ns	ns	ns	ns
Punitiveness	ns	ns	ns	ns
Permissiveness	ns	ns	ns	ns
Detachment	ns	ns	ns	ns

---

[16] ANOVA looks at whether there are any significant differences in means between any of the four change categories.

Table 2A.4 Mean scores on quality of pre-school centre and children's levels of 'risk' across three time points for social/behavioural outcomes

Emotional symptoms	'at risk' only at entry to the study	'at risk' two time points	Always 'at risk'	Anova
ECERS-R	ns	ns	ns	ns
ECERS-E	ns	ns	ns	ns
CIS				
Positive relationship	ns	ns	ns	ns
Punitiveness	ns	ns	ns	ns
Permissiveness	ns	ns	ns	ns
Detachment	ns	ns	ns	ns
Conduct problems	'at risk' only at entry to the study	'at risk' two time points	Always 'at risk'	Anova[17]
ECERS-R	ns	ns	ns	ns
ECERS-E	3.08 (0.94)	3.39 (0.98)	3.05 (0.93)	P<0.05
CIS				
Positive relationship	3.23 (0.49)	3.39 (0.46)	3.20 (0.49)	p<0.01
Punitiveness	ns	ns	ns	ns
Permissiveness	ns	ns	ns	ns
Detachment	1.42 (0.47)	1.33 (0.44)	1.56 (0.51)	p<0.01
Peer problems	'at risk" only at entry to the study	'at risk' two time points	Always 'at risk'	Anova[18]
ECERS-R	ns	ns	ns	ns
ECERS-E	ns	ns	ns	ns
CIS				
Positive relationship	ns	ns	ns	ns
Punitiveness	ns	ns	ns	ns
Permissiveness	ns	ns	ns	ns
Detachment	1.36 (0.40)	1.44 (0.52)	1.57 (0.58)	p<0.05

( ) Standard deviation
ns not statistically significant

Assessing the impact of pre-school quality on Year 1 outcomes after controlling for pupil background of Year 1 assessments

Background details about children's earlier childcare experiences, health, family and 'home' learning environment were obtained from parental interviews conducted when children entered the EPPE study. It is important to control for differences in attainment attributable to a child's background before we can investigate whether pre-school quality is associated with better academic performance and more positive social behavioural outcomes at the end of Year 1.

Section 1C has outlined some of the findings from the complex multilevel models used to explore the impact of background. EYTSEN Technical Paper 1 reported findings from multilevel analyses of children's progress (attainment gains taking account of prior attainment at the start of pre-school) over the pre-school period, and found that children attending higher quality pre-schools had made more progress over the pre-school period than those attending lower quality centres.

The results of analyses of children's attainment at the end of Year 1 in Reading indicate that some aspects of pre-school centre quality also continue to show a significant positive association with attainment at this later age (6 years plus), even when differences in children's background

---

[17] ANOVA looks at whether there are any significant differences in means between any of the four change categories.
[18] ANOVA looks at whether there are any significant differences in means between any of the four change categories.

characteristics are controlled (see Appendix 5 for details of the contextualised multilevel models). Children who had attended higher quality settings continued to attain significantly higher Reading scores. It has already been shown that higher quality pre-school experiences were related to better outcomes at the start of primary school (see figures in EYTSEN Technical Paper 1). For Reading the Literacy subscale from ECERS-E, the total ECERS-R and the CIS Positive relationships scales all showed a significant association with better outcomes. These results confirm that the quality of pre-school experience continues to influence child outcomes during Key stage 1. From this we can conclude that those who did not attend pre-school (the 'home' group), or who attended lower quality provision are at a disadvantage compared with other children.

Measures of the effectiveness (in promoting cognitive gains over the pre-school period) of the pre-school setting were also calculated. These showed a significant positive association with subsequent mathematics attainment in Key Stage 1 (Year 1). In addition, there were indications that the effectiveness of the pre-school setting in promoting language and pre-Reading skills was also associated with better reading attainment at the end of Year 1.

Elsewhere it has been shown that quality and effectiveness are linked. The observed quality of pre-school settings was associated with greater effectiveness in promoting young children's cognitive progress during the pre-school period (see EPPE Technical Papers 8a and 8b). These results support the view that quality and effectiveness of pre-school settings continue to influence young children's attainments in the first years of primary school.

SUMMARY AND CONCLUSION

The main focus of the EYTSEN study has been the identification of young children who may be seen as 'at risk' of SEN on the basis of lower cognitive scores or less favourable social/behavioural development profiles at three time points: entry to the pre-school study (age 3 years plus), entry to primary school (rising 5 years) and at the end of Year 1 (age 6 years plus). The analyses show consistent links between particular child, family and home learning characteristics and 'at risk' status. The incidence of multiple disadvantage is particularly influential. This supports the view that SEN may be influenced by both personal and environmental factors and that some environments may ameliorate while others may be seen to exacerbate SEN. The EYTSEN research points to factors which can be seen to offer protection and others which by contrast increase the 'risk' of SEN and may be interpreted in terms of resiliency and vulnerability.

The research has examined the characteristics of children reported by teachers to show some form of SEN at primary school. This includes children receiving any form of support and those with more extreme needs who have been statemented. The characteristics of children identified by schools as showing SEN were very similar to those of children classified as 'at risk' using the EYTSEN criteria. There was also considerable overlap between the identification of children 'at risk' by the research, and those reported to have SEN at school. This overlap was greater for cognitive outcomes than social behaviour. This suggests that the use of 'at risk' approaches may help in the early identification of SEN in pre-school or reception and thus enabling support to be targeted at an early stage.

A number of key findings emerge from the EYTSEN research and are reported in this EYTSEN Technical Paper (for Key Stage 1) or EYTSEN Technical Paper 1 (for the pre-school period).

- Identifying the characteristics of children 'at risk' of SEN at three separate time points reveals that this group of children have particular characteristics that remain relatively stable over the three time points. For example, children 'at risk' for cognitive outcomes are of low birthweight, have mothers with no qualifications, mothers not working and fathers in lower SES occupations. Children 'at risk' were also more likely to have poorer home learning environments. Although the strength of this last relationship is greatest at entry to pre-school and appears to diminish as children move through the first years of primary school it remains a significant factor at the end of Year 1. We can conclude that a child's home learning environment at entry to the study (age 3 years plus) remains a useful single predictor of the likelihood of being identified as 'at risk' at the end of Year 1.

- A multiple disadvantage index was created based on 10 individual indicators, each found to be related to 'at risk' status when tested separately. This index, based on data collected at entry to the study remains an important predictor of 'at risk' status at the end of Year 1. The results suggest that multiple disadvantage is a consistent predictor of 'at risk' status, and it is a more powerful indicator than any of the individual 'risk' factors alone.

- 'Home' children were found to experience greater multiple disadvantage levels than those in the pre-school sample, even when this was controlled, they were more likely to be 'at risk' and to be reported by teachers as showing some form of SEN at primary school.

- Gender and English as an additional language (EAL) status are two child characteristics of particular interest. At the end of Year 1, boys were more likely to be identified as 'at risk' for reading and mathematics attainments and also for, Peer problems and especially Conduct problems. The gap appears to be already in place by entry to primary school, and analyses of pupil progress over the pre-school period show that girls made significantly more progress in Pre-Reading, Early number concepts and Non-verbal outcomes than the boys (See EPPE Technical Paper 8a for more details). This suggests that gender differences appear very early during the pre-school years, so that interventions seeking to combat gender difference need to be put in place before the start of primary school.

- Although EAL children were still more likely to be identified as 'at risk' for reading and Mathematics in Year 1, they were no longer more likely to be 'at risk' on any of the social/behavioural outcomes by the end of Year 1. Analyses of pupil progress suggest that this group of children tended to narrow the gap with non-EAL children for Pre-Reading skills in the pre-school period, but no further narrowing of the gap was evident in the early primary school years.

- The link between cognitive difficulties and child behaviour as rated by pre-school staff or later by class teachers at school was assessed at each time point. The findings suggest that behavioural problems can co-exist with cognitive difficulties in over two thirds of children (at the end of Year 1), although the type of behavioural problem can vary quite widely.

- The finding that significantly more summer born children (those young for their school year) are reported by schools as showing SEN is also of concern. Research on junior schools in the 1980s found that teachers judged pupils young for their year as of lower ability than their older peers and having more behaviour problems (Mortimore et al, 1988). The EYTSEN findings from a national sample 20 years on indicate that summer born children remain at a disadvantage and are more likely to be viewed as having some form of SEN. The results suggest the need to raise awareness of the impact of developmental age and to ensure that children young for their year receive more support without lowering expectations. The EYTSEN research used age standardised scores and identified children 'at risk' of SEN as those who scored below a particular 'cut off'. Such an approach could assist schools to adopt a more systematic approach and avoid the bias in identification towards those young for their year.

- One of the main purposes of the project was to investigate the impact of pre-school on 'at risk' status. EYTSEN Technical Paper 1 investigated this issue in some detail and found that Integrated centres and nursery schools were much more likely to serve vulnerable children (as measured by 'at risk' status at entry to the study), reflecting the tendency for them to be located in areas of high disadvantage. However, these types of provision were also more likely to take children out of 'risk' classification.

- It was also found that the incidence of 'risk' (measured by low cognitive scores in relation to national norms) was reduced from one third to one fifth over the pre-school period for the sample of pre-school children in the study, suggesting that pre-school itself has a significant positive impact on young children's cognitive outcomes. Some types of provision appeared to be particularly beneficial. This conclusion was supported by analyses of data for 'home' children (pupils who had no pre-school experience before starting primary school). Analyses for the main EPPE study (reported in EPPE Technical Papers 8a and 8b) show that, even taking into account the important differences in background between the 'pre-school' and the 'home' sample, the 'home' sample have significantly poorer scores in Pre-Reading, Early Number Concepts and Language development when starting school. We might expect that this group of children would make more progress than the pre-school group in the first years of primary school as they catch up. However, this was not found in the analyses of cognitive and behavioural gains over the first two years of primary school. This suggests that additional intervention may be needed to help such children to catch up with the pre-school group.

- Further analyses at the end of Year 1 have shown that particular aspects of pre-school quality appear to have an enduring influence on pupil attainment and behaviour. A high quality literacy curriculum within the pre-school, as measured by the ECERS-E instrument is related to better attainment at the end of Year 1 in Reading. Children who had attended pre-schools that promoted progress in Early Number concepts scored significantly higher than other children in Mathematics attainment in Year 1. Children from centres that were more effective at promoting progress during the pre-school period were still ahead of other children by the end of Year 1. Similarly, children from centres that promoted progress in Antisocial/worried/upset outcome were showing significantly better Peer and Conduct behaviours than other children at this time point.

Taken together, the EYTSEN results indicate that pre-school itself can be seen as an effective intervention which reduces the 'risk' of SEN especially for vulnerable children, including those with multiple disadvantage. 'Home' children (who had not attended a pre-school centre) were much more likely to be identified as 'at risk' at the start of primary school than other children. This was the case even when level of multiple disadvantage is controlled. 'Home' children were also more likely to be reported subsequently as having a SEN by teachers at school. The absence of pre-school can be seen as an additional disadvantage for the most vulnerable groups of young children. The positive impact of pre-school in reducing the 'risk' of SEN remains evident at the end of Year 1.

References

American Psychiatric Association (1994) *Diagnostic and statistical manual of mental disorders (4th ed)*. Washington, D.C: Author.

Arnett, J. (1989) Caregivers in Day-Care Centres: Does training matter? *Journal of Applied Developmental Psychology*, 10, 541-552.

DfES (2001) Special Educational Needs : Code of Practice. London. DfES.

Department for Education and Skills (2002) *National statistics Bulletin: Statistics of Education Special Educational Needs in England January 2002*. Issue 10/02.

Department for Education and Skills (2003) *National statistics First release: Pupil characteristics and class sizes in maintained schools in England January 2003 (provisional)*. Issue 09/03.

Elliot, C., with Smith, P. and McCulloch, K. (1996), *British Ability Scales Second Edition (BAS II)*. Windsor: NFER-Nelson Publishing Company Limited.

France, N. NFER-NELSON. (1978), *Primary Reading Test Level 1*. Windsor: NFER-NELSON Publishing Company Ltd.

Goodman, R (1997) The Strengths and Difficulties Questionnaire: A Research Note, *Journal of Psychology and Psychiatry*, Vol 38, No 5, pg 581-586.

Goodman, R & Scott, S (1999) Comparing the Strengths and Difficulties Questionnaire and the Child Behavior Checklist: Is Small Beautiful? *Journal of Abnormal Child Psychology*, Vol 27, No 1, pg 17-24.

Goodman, R, Ford, T, Simmons, H, Gatward, R & Meltzer, H (2000a) Using the Strengths and Difficulties Questionnaire (SDQ) to screen for child psychiatric disorder in a community sample, British Journal of Psychiatry, 177, pg 534-539.

Goodman, R, Renfrew, D, & Mullick, M (2000b) Predicting type of psychiatric disorder from Strengths and Difficulties (SDQ) scores in child mental health clinics in London and Daka, European Child and Adolescent Psychiatry, 9, pg 129-134.

Hagues, N., Caspall, L., & Clayden, H. NFER-NELSON and with Patilla, P. (1997), *Mathematics 6*. Windsor: NFER-NELSON Publishing Company Ltd.

Harms, T., Clifford, M. and Cryer, D. (1998), *Early Childhood Environment Rating Scale, Revised Edition (ECERS-R)*. Vermont: Teachers College Press.

Hay, D, Pawlby, S, Sharp, D, & Schmucker, G, Mills, A, Allen, H & Kumar, R (1999) Parents' Judgements About Young Children's Problems: Why Mothers and Fathers Might Disagree Yet Still Predict Later Outcomes, *Journal of Child Psychology and Psychiatry*, Vol 40, No 8, pg 1249-1258.

Heiser, A., Curcin, O., Luhr, C., Metze, B and Obladen, M (2000) Parental and professional agreement in development assessment of very-low-birthweight and term infants, *Developmental Medicine and Child Neurology*, 42, 21-24.

Hogan, A.E, Scott, K.G, Bauer, C.R (1992) The Adaptive Social Behaviour Inventory (ASBI): A new assessment of social competence in high risk three year olds, *Journal of Psychoeducational Assessments*, 10 (3), pg 230-239.

Meltzer, H., Gatward, R., Goodman, R., and Ford, F. (2000) *Mental health of children and adolescents in Great Britain*. London: The Stationery Office.

Mortimore, P, Sammons, P, Stoll, L, Lewis, D & Ecob, R (1988) *School Matters: the Junior Years,* Wells: Open Books.

Plomin, R, Price, T, Eley, T, Dale, P, & Stevenson, J (2002) Associations between behaviour problems and verbal and nonverbal cognitive abilities and disabilities in early childhood, *Journal of Child Psychology and Psychiatry*, 43:5, pg 619-633.

Roffey, S (1999*) Special Needs in the Early Years: Collaboration, Communication and Co-ordination.* David Fulton: London.

Sonuga-Barke, E, Lamparelli, M, Stevenson, J, Thompson, M & Henry, A (1994) Behaviour problems and pre-school Intellectual attainment: The associations of Hyperactivity and Conduct problems, Journal of Child Psychology and Psychiatry, Vol 35, No5, pg 949-960.

Scott & Carran (1989) Identification and Referral of Handicapped Infants, in Wang, M.C, Reynolds, M.C & Walberg, H.J (eds) *Handbook of Special Education Research and Practice*, Volume 3, Low Incidence Conditions, pg
227-242

Sylva, K, Taggart, B, Melhuish, E, Sammons, P & Siraj-Blatchford, I (1999) *The Effective Provision of Pre-School Education [EPPE] Project A longitudinal Study funded by the DfEE (1997-2003). Tender Submission for Early Years Transitions and Special Educational Needs (EYTSEN).* Department for Education and Employment Tender No 4/RP/167/2000

Sylva, K., Siraj-Blatchford, I. and Taggart, B. (2003), *Assessing Quality in the Early Years Early Childhood Environment Rating Scale Extension (ECERS-E): Four Curricular Subscales.* Stoke on Trent: Trentham Books.

White, J.L, Moffitt, T.E, Earls, F, Robins, L, & Silva, P.A (1990) How early can we tell? Predictors of childhood conduct disorder and adolescent delinquency, *Criminology*, 28, pg 507-533.

World Health Organization (1994) *The ICD-10 classification of mental and behavioural disorders: Diagnostic criteria for research.* Geneva, Switzerland: World Health Organization.

APPENDIX 1: EYTSEN TECHNICAL PAPERS

EYTSEN Technical Paper 1: Special Educational Needs across the Pre-school Period

EYTSEN Technical Paper 2: Special Educational Needs in the Early Primary Years: Primary School entry up to the end of Year 1.

EYTSEN Technical Paper 3: Special Educational Needs in the Early Years: The Parents' Perspective

The Early Years Transition and Special Educational Needs (EYTSEN) Project Research Brief No. 431RB, July 2003 ISBN 1 84478 021 X

The Early Years Transition and Special Educational Needs (EYTSEN) Project Research Report No. 431RR, July 2003 ISBN 1 84185 021X

APPENDIX 2: The Effective Provision of Pre-School (EPPE) Project Technical Papers

Technical Paper 1 - An Introduction to the Effective Provision of Pre-school Education (EPPE) Project ISBN: 085473 591 7   Published: Autumn 1999   Price £8.50

Technical Paper 2 - Characteristics of the Effective Provision of Pre-School Education (EPPE) Project sample at entry to the study
ISBN: 085473 592 5   Published: Autumn 1999   Price £4.00

Technical Paper 3 - Contextualising EPPE: Interviews with Local Authority co-ordinators and centre managers
ISBN: 085473 593 3   Published: Autumn 1999   Price £3.50

Technical Paper 4 - Parent, family and child characteristics in relation to type of pre-school and socio-economic differences.
ISBN: 085473 594 1   Published: Autumn 1999   Price £4.00

Technical Paper 5 – Characteristics of the Centre in the EPPE Study: (Interviews)
ISBN: 085473 595 X   Published: Autumn 2000   Price £5.00

Technical Paper 6 - Characteristics of the Centres in the EPPE Sample: Observational Profiles
ISBN: 085473 596 8   Published: Autumn 1999   Price £8.50

Technical Paper 6A - Characteristics of Pre-School Environments
ISBN: 085473 597 6   Published: Autumn 1999   Price £8.50

Technical Paper 7 - Social/behavioural and cognitive development at 3-4 years in relation to family background   ISBN: 085473 598 4   Published: Spring 2001   Price £5.00

Technical Paper 8a – Measuring the Impact of Pre-School on Children's Cognitive Progress over the Pre-School Period. ISBN: 085473 599 2   Published: Autumn 2002   Price £8.50

Technical Paper 8b – Measuring the Impact of Pre-School on Children's Social/behavioural Development over the Pre-School Period.
ISBN: 085473 683 2   Published March 2003   Price £8.50

Technical Paper 9 - Report on age 6 assessment
ISBN: 085473 600 X   Publication Date: Autumn 2004

Technical Paper 10 - Intensive study of selected centres
ISBN: 085473 601 8   Published November 2003 Price £11.00

Technical Paper 11 - Report on the continuing effects of pre-school education at age 7
ISBN: 085473 602 6   Publication Date: Autumn 2004

Technical Paper 12 - The final report   ISBN: 085473 603 4   Publication Date: Autumn 2004

Ordering information Visit the EPPE Website http://www.ioe.ac.uk/projects/eppe

The Bookshop at the Institute of Education. 20, Bedford Way. London WC1H OAL. Tele: 00 44 (0) 207 612 6050 Fax: 0207 612 6407 e-mail: ioe@johnsmith.co.uk, website: www.johnsmith.co.uk/ioe or   The EPPE Office. The University of London, Institute of Education. 20 Bedford Way, London. WC1H OAL. U.K. Telephone 00 44 (0) 207 612 6219 / Fax. 00 44 (0) 207 612 6230 / e-mail b.taggart@ioe.ac.uk

Appendix 3 – Child assessments

The Early Childhood Environment Rating Scale: Revised Edition (1998). Harms, Clifford and Cryer ISBN: 08077 3751 8 Available from Teachers College Press. Columbia University. 1234 Amsterdam Avenue. New York. NY10027

The Early Childhood Environment Rating Scale: ECERS-E (2003) Sylva, Siraj-Blatchford and Taggart (in press) on publication available from Trentham Books
Early Years Transition and Special Educational Needs (EYTSEN) Technical Paper 1: Special Educational Needs across the Pre-school Period.

Four common points of assessment were used in the EPPE study:

- **Entry to pre school study**

Table A2.1 Entry to Target Pre-school assessments (age 3.0 to 4 years 3 months)

Name of Assessment	Assessment Content	Administered by:
British Ability Scales Second Edition (BASII) (Elliot et al., 1996): • Block Building • Verbal Comprehension • Picture Similarity • Naming Vocabulary	Cognitive development battery • Spatial skills • Verbal skills • Pictorial reasoning skills • Verbal skills	 EPPE Researcher EPPE Researcher EPPE Researcher EPPE Researcher
Adaptive Social Behavioural Inventory (ASBI) (Hogan et al., 1992)	Social behaviour and emotional adjustment	Centre Staff
Children not fluent in English: Assessed only on the non-verbal BAS II scales (Block Building and Picture Similarity) and social and emotional behaviour.		

These assessments were chosen to provide a baseline against which later progress and development can be compared. The British Ability Scales (BAS sub-scales) are designed for use with this age range. Research Officers in each region were trained in their use and checked for reliability. They assessed children on a one-to-one basis. Where possible an interpreter was recruited who spoke the child's 'home' language if the child was not fluent in English. Centre staff that were familiar with the child completed an Adaptive Social Behaviour Inventory (ASBI) for each sample child to provide a measure of social and behavioural development.

Entry to primary school (age rising 5 years)

All children were assessed at entry to school (usually at the start of reception, though some children went straight into a Year 1 class). These assessments provide both a measure of current attainment and development at exit from pre-school and serve as a baseline for entry to school. The assessments were chosen to be compatible with the Desirable Outcomes for Pre-School Education (DfEE, 1996).

Table A2.2 Entry to Target primary school assessments

Name of Assessment	Assessment Content	Administered by:
British Ability Scales Second Edition (BASII) (Elliot et al., 1996): • Verbal Comprehension • Picture Similarity • Naming Vocabulary • Pattern Construction	Cognitive development battery • Verbal skills • Pictorial reasoning skills • Verbal skills • Spatial skills	 EPPE Researcher EPPE Researcher EPPE Researcher EPPE Researcher
BAS Early Number Concepts	Reasoning ability	EPPE Researcher
Letter Recognition	Lower case letters	EPPE Researcher

Phonological Awareness (Bryant and Bradley, 1985)	Rhyme and Alliteration	EPPE Researcher
Adaptive Social Behavioural Inventory (ASBI - R) (Hogan et al., 1992)	Social and emotional behaviour, hyperactivity and settling-into-school	Class Teacher

Children not fluent in English: Assessed only on two of the non-verbal BAS II scales (Picture Similarity and Pattern Construction) and social behaviour. In addition they were assessed on BAS II Copying, a measure of spatial ability, (Elliot et al., 1996), which was also administered by the EPPE researcher.

The ASBI was also adapted and extended by the EPPE team to cover a greater range of behaviours considered appropriate for school age children by incorporating selected additional items from other published tests, covering hyperactivity and prosocial behaviour.

- **End of Year 1 in Primary**

Table A2.4 Outcome measures at age 6 plus include:

Name of Assessment	Assessment Content	Administered by:
Primary Reading: Level 1 (NFER-Nelson)		Class Teacher
Mathematics 6 (NFER-Nelson)		Class Teacher
Strengths and Difficulties Questionnaire (Goodman, 1997) for extended study	Hyperactivity, Conduct problems, peer problems, emotional problems and prosocial	Class Teacher

- **End of Year 2 in Primary**

Table A2.5 Outcome measures at age 7 plus include:

Name of Assessment	Assessment Content	Administered by:
Strengths and Difficulties Questionnaire (Goodman, 1997) extended for study	Hyperactivity, Conduct problems, peer problems, emotional problems and pro-social	Class Teacher
Attitudes to School Questionnaire	Children's views on academic and social activities	Completed by child
Record of conduct / emotional problems		From school records
National Assessments	Reading, Writing and Mathematics: National Assessments Science: teacher assessed	From school records

Appendix 4 – Items included in the Goodman Strengths and Difficulties Questionnaire scales

The 'Prosocial' scale
Considerate of other people's feelings
Shares readily with other children
Helpful if someone is hurt, upset or feeling ill
Kind to younger children
Often volunteers to help others

The 'Hyperactivity' scale
Restless, overactive, cannot stay still for long
Constantly fidgeting or squirming
Easily distracted, concentration wanders
Thinks things out before acting
Sees tasks through to the end before acting

The 'Emotional symptoms' scale
Often complains of headaches, stomach-aches…
Many worries, often seems worried
Often unhappy, downhearted or tearful
Nervous or clingy in new situations….
Many fears, easily scared

The 'Conduct problems' scale
Often has temper tantrums or hot tempers
Generally obedient, usually does what he/she is told
Often fights with other children or bullies them
Often lies or cheats

The 'Peer problems' scale
Rather solitary, tends to play alone
Has at least one good friend
Generally liked by other children
Picked on or bullied by other children
Gets on better with adults than with children

Many of the items have reverse scoring where there is a mixture of positive and negative statements within the scale

Appendix 5 – Significance of pre-school quality indicators after controlling for pupil background at the end of Year 1

Table A5.1 Quality of pre-school and cognitive outcomes at the end of Year 1

Tested individually	Year 1 outcomes				
	Reading	Mathematics	Emotional symptoms	Conduct Problems	Peer Problems
Value Added scores:					
Early Number concepts	0.033+	0.001+			
Pattern construction	ns	0.009+			
Picture similarities	ns	ns			
Pre-Reading	0.054+	Ns			
Total verbal	0.002+	0.02+			
Co-operation & conformity			0.05+	0.000+	0.036+
Independence & concentration			ns	0.001+	ns
Peer sociability			0.015+	0.013+	ns
Anti-social /worried upset**			ns	0.001-	0.022-
ECERS-R – overall	0.001+	ns	ns	ns	ns
ECERS-E – overall	0.004+	ns	ns	ns	ns
ECERS E & R – individual					
space and furnishings items 1 - 8	0.006+	ns	ns	0.026+	ns
personal care routines items 9 - 14	0.01+	ns	ns	ns	ns
language reasoning items 15-18	0.04+	ns	ns	0.028+	ns
activities items 19 – 28	0.01+	ns	ns	ns	ns
interaction items 29 – 33	0.01+	ns	ns	0.014+	0.040+
programme structure items 34 - 37	0.04+	ns	ns	ns	ns
parents and staff items 38 - 43	ns	ns	ns	ns	ns
literacy subscale items 1 - 6	0.000+	ns	ns	ns	ns
Mathematics subscale items 1 - 4	0.04+	ns	ns	ns	ns
science and environment items 1- 5	0.02+	ns	ns	ns	ns
diversity subscale items 1 - 3	ns	0.04-	ns	ns	ns
CIS:					
Positive relationship	0.007+	ns	0.053+	ns	ns
Punitiveness	ns	ns	ns	ns	ns
Permissiveness	ns	ns	ns	ns	ns
Detachment	ns	ns	ns	ns	ns
Significant when tested together	Literacy	Early Number concepts Diversity	none	Anti-social /worried upset	Anti-social /worried upset

** A positive score represents a negative outcome

49

Glossary of terms

Age standardised scores – Assessment scores that have been adjusted to take account of the child's age at time of testing.

Anti-social/worried – This is measured on the ASBI scale (see social/ behavioural development in this glossary. Items on the scale, which identify anti-social behaviour, would be: teases other children, calls them names.

'at risk' – The report acknowledges that the term 'at risk' is a complex one, which will differ depending on the particular criteria used. In this study we have referred to **cognitive 'risk'** (1 sd below national average) and '**strong cognitive risk'** (1 sd below sample average). These provide definitions of children who may be seen to be 'at risk' on the basis of their cognitive attainment at entry to pre-school. For social/behavioural 'at risk' we use one standard deviation below the mean for the sample, as measure on the ASBI (see social/behavioural in this glossary) as a cut off (see cut off in this glossary) for the factors, Anti-social/worried/ upset and Peer sociability. The EPPE definitions of 'at risk' (using standardised assessments) could therefore be said to be 'actual' rather than 'perceptual' 'risk'. However, the views of parents, pre-school workers and teachers about whether or not a child falls into an 'at risk' category are based more on 'perceptual' than 'actual' 'risk'.

British Ability Scales (BAS) – This is a battery of assessments specially developed by NFER/Nelson to assess very young children's abilities. The assessments used at entry and end of pre-school were:
Block building - which measures Visual-perceptual matching, especially in spatial orientation
Naming Vocabulary – Expressive language and knowledge of names
Pattern construction – Non-verbal reasoning and spatial visualisation
Picture Similarities – Non-verbal reasoning
Early number concepts – Knowledge of, and problem solving using pre-numerical and numerical concepts.
Copying – Visual-perceptual matching and fine-motor co-ordination. Used specifically for children with English as an additional language or who are not fluent in English.
Verbal comprehension – Receptive language: understanding of oral instructions involving basic language concepts.

The Caregiver Interaction Scale (CIS) is a rating scale consisting of 26 items completed by an observer of the interactions between caregivers and children. The items are grouped to produce 4 subscales, scored from one to four: positive relationships, punitiveness, permissiveness and detachment.
- Positive relationships is a subscale made up of 10 items indicating warmth and enthusiasm interaction with children by the caregiver.
- Punitiveness is a subscale made up of 8 items indicating harsh or over-controlling behaviour in interaction with children by the caregiver.
- Permissiveness is a subscale made up of 4 items indicating avoidance of discipline and control of children by the caregiver.
- Detachment is a subscale made up of 4 items indicating lack of involvement in interaction with children by the caregiver.

Child/parent factors – Examples of child factors would be gender, ethnicity etc. Examples of parent factors would be mother's qualifications and father's employment.

Cognitive development – Children's intellectual and conceptual development, measured on the EPPE project by assessments which quantified: Verbal Ability, Non-verbal Ability and Spatial Ability, at entry to Pre- school. Subsequent assessments measure children's pre-Reading abilities, phonological awareness (knowledge of alphabetic sounds) and number awareness. For information on assessments see British Ability Scales in this glossary.

Cut off – The score below which children are deemed to be 'at risk', 1 standard deviation below the mean (see standard deviation in this glossary).

The Early Childhood Environment Rating Scale – Revised (ECERS-R) is a rating scale consisting of 43 items completed by an observer that assesses the overall quality of the childhood setting. The items are grouped to produce 7 subscales: space and furnishings, personal care practices, language and reasoning, pre-school activities, social interaction, organization and routines, adults working together.

The Early Childhood Environment Rating Scale – Extension (ECERS-E) is a new rating scale developed specifically for the EPPE project to supplement the ECERS-R consisting of 18 items. It is based on the Desirable Learning Outcomes for 3 and 4 year olds and pedagogical practices associated with it and consists of items completed by an observer of the childhood setting's activities. The items are grouped to produce 4 subscales: literacy, Mathematics, science/environment, and diversity.

General Cognitive Ability (GCA) – a measure of children's overall cognitive ability, incorporating non-verbal and verbal BAS subscales. At entry to the study the BAS subscales that made up the 'GCA' were: Block Building, Naming Vocabulary, Picture Similarities and Verbal Comprehension. At entry to Primary School, 'GCA' was made from Naming Vocabulary, Picture Similarities, Verbal Comprehension, Early Number Concepts and Pattern Construction. (See cognitive development and British Ability Scales in this glossary).

Goodman Strengths and Difficulties Questionnaire (SDQ)
(Goodman, 1997) is made up of five sub-scales: Pro-social, hyperactivity, emotional problems, and Peer sociability.

'Home' learning environment – A composite score derived from reports from parents (at interview) about what children do at 'home', combining seven types of 'home' learning activities; Reading, library visits, playing with letters or numbers, painting and drawing, playing/teaching alphabet or letters, playing/teaching with numbers/shapes and playing/teaching of songs/nursery rhymes. The composite score identifies households that have a rich or more impoverished 'home' learning environment for children.

Intervention study – This is a study in which researchers 'intervene' in the sample to control variables i.e. control by setting the adult/child ratios in order to compare different specific ratios in different settings. EPPE is not an intervention study in that it investigates naturally occurring variation in pre-school settings.

Peer sociability – This is the ability to 'get on' with other children. It is an important milestone in young children's social development and includes the ability to empathise, sympathise and relate to peers. Children with poor Peer sociability can often be withdrawn and isolate. Examples of Peer sociability on our rating scale were: willing to join a group of children playing, understands others' feeling, like when they are happy, sad or mad, asks or wants to go and play with other children etc.

Multiple Disadvantage Index (MDI) – An index based on three child variables, six parent variables, and one related to the 'home' learning environment which were considered 'risk' indicators when looked at in isolation. A child's MDI was calculated by summing the number of indicators the child was 'at risk' on.

Sampling profile/procedures – The EPPE sample was constructed by:

Five regions (six LEAs) randomly selected around the country, but being representative of urban, rural, inner city areas.

Pre-schools from each of the 6 types of target provision (nursery classes, nursery schools, Local authority day nurseries private day nurseries, play groups and combined centres) randomly selected across the region.

Children randomly selected within each target centre, of the required age that met criteria for eligibility (i.e. assessed within 10 weeks of entry if over 3, assessed just after third birthday if already at centre at a younger age).

Social/behavioural development – By this we mean a child's ability to 'socialise' with other adults and children and their general behaviour to others. EPPE, unlike other studies, has considered both social and cognitive development of young children. Children's social/behavioural development considers children's social competence, pro-social behaviour (social skills) and anti-social behaviour. Social/behavioural development is measured by the Adaptive Social Behavioural Inventory (ASBI), specifically developed for very young children's behaviour at entry to pre-school. Subsequent assessments measure any peers and emotional problems children may be experiencing.

Special Non-verbal Composite (SNC) - Created from the non-verbal BAS scores (see British Ability Scales in this glossary).

Standard deviation – A measure of the spread around the mean. In a normal distribution 68 percent of cases fall within one, plus or minus standard deviation of the mean and 95 percent of case fall within two standard deviations.

Stress factor loading – Level of perceived stress associated with a particular life event i.e. divorce, bereavement, taken from McCubbin, H., and Patterson J. (1991) (see reference section of this report).

Value added analyses of progress

The analyses use statistical (multilevel) models to explore individual children's progress over time and variations in centre effectiveness, taking account of their prior attainment at entry to pre-school using attainments at entry to primary school as outcomes.